THE SCIENCE OF ACHIEVING YOUR DESIRES

DR. RUBY LALRINSANGI

Made with ♥ on the Notion Press Platform
www.notionpress.com

Contents

ACKNOWLEDGEMENTS

I want to take a moment to give the universe my sincere thanks for lining up the stars and leading me to this time. Your enigmatic ways have taught me that anything is possible if one has faith, works hard, and is determined.

Thank you, God, for all of the blessings, good health, inspiration, and love that you have bestowed upon me over the course of my life. I have always had your support and advice at my side, and I will always be grateful for your kindness and your unbounded knowledge.

Thank you to my mother and family for always having faith in me despite my own doubts. I am very blessed to have you in my life since your everlasting love and support have been the cornerstone of my success.

I want to thank my friends for their support, encouragement, and faith in me. I am grateful to have you all in my life since your friendship has been a constant source of happiness and inspiration.

I want to express my sincere gratitude to everyone who is reading my book. More than words can say, I genuinely appreciate your support and the time, interest, and curiosity you have shown in my work; Words cannot express how grateful I am. The labor of love that goes into writing a book feels significant and deserving because of readers like you. I send you blessings, long-lasting joy, and success in all your endeavors. Because that's what I want to do most of all as an author, I'm humbled by the thought that my words can resonate with you as a reader.

Finally, I'd like to express my gratitude to everyone who has supported and encouraged me along the path. I am incredibly appreciative of the part you have played in my path. Your efforts, both large and small, have helped mold me into the person I am today.

INTRODUCTION

Dear readers,

Do you want to live the life of your dreams and fulfill your deepest desires? Are you curious to find out how to apply the science of manifestation to create the reality you desire? If so, then this book is for you.

My own journey with manifestation began when I was experiencing a sense of stagnation and unhappiness in both my personal and professional lives. I had a job that didn't motivate me. I felt as though I was just going through the motions every day without any sense of purpose or direction because I was in a relationship that wasn't emotionally fulfilling.

I began to investigate various methods for personal growth at this time, such as meditation, visualization, and affirmations. I started concentrating on what I really desired in life, and I began to picture myself leading that life.

I was astounded by the outcomes I started to observe. Opportunities that I had never considered becoming available to me began to appear overnight. I cleared the NET JRF exam, got a Ph.D. admission into my dream University by topping the entrance, and manifested the most loving and fulfilling relationship. I started to meet people who could assist me in achieving my objectives, and I started to feel more self-assured and inspired to take steps in the direction of my ambitions.

I became more and more curious about the science of manifestation as my own experiences with it developed. I was curious as to what actually occurred when we make intentions and see the results we want.

I therefore committed myself to learning about the most recent studies on manifestation, as well as investigating the ideas of old wisdom traditions and personal development. I gained knowledge of the brain's potential, the function of energy fields, and the study of intentions.

I gained a deeper understanding of how manifestation functions and how we can use it to design the life we want via my studies. Through "The Science of Achieving Your Desires," I now wish to spread this information to others.

The result of years of study and personal experience, this book is meant to assist readers in harnessing the power of manifestation and realizing their own aspirations. This book will provide you with the skills and information you need to realize your greatest aspirations, whether you want to enhance your health, relationships, profession, or any other area of your life.

You'll discover the most recent findings in scientific studies on manifestation in this book, including information on the brain's function, energy fields, and the influence of purpose. Additionally, you will learn how to make specific goals, visualize your desired results, and develop a positive outlook to help your manifestation journey.

"The Science of Achieving Your Desires" will undoubtedly be a useful tool for everyone interested in personal development, in my opinion. I therefore ask you to embark on this voyage of discovery and transformation with me if you are prepared to take charge of your life and begin fulfilling your dreams.

I
Gratitude As a Magnet

Understanding Gratitude

Gratitude is a state of mind in which one feels thankful for the good things in one's life, situations, and experiences. No matter how small or significant they may be, it is noticing and appreciating the wonderful things that occur to you or the positive parts of your life. It is possible to nurture and practice gratitude as an attitude that can help you in achieving your desires, be it relationships, health, or wealth.

People frequently express their gratitude to others by thanking them for acts of generosity or support from friends, family, coworkers, or even complete strangers. It can also be addressed to oneself in order to acknowledge one's own successes, qualities, and efforts. Verbally expressing gratitude, writing thank-you cards, performing deeds of kindness, or simply thinking about the good things in life are all examples of how gratitude can be communicated.

It has been demonstrated that cultivating thankfulness has a wide range of positive effects, including enhancements to relationships, mental and physical health, happiness, and well-being. Gratitude can help people change their perspective from what they don't have in life to what they do have, and it can promote a grateful attitude. It can be developed via intentional practice, awareness, and contemplation and is a potent tool for improving one's emotional and mental health.

Gratitude: A Science?

"Yes! You get it right. Gratitude is one of the most effective methods for attaining your goals scientifically. According to science, one of the major emotions that can connect your thoughts and emotions with positive energy and improve the efficacy of attaining your life's goals is gratitude."

Your attention will change from what you lack to what you already have when you are grateful. You are turning your focus in the direction of prosperity and positivity by recognizing and appreciating the benefits, successes, and positive aspects of your life. You can attract more fulfilling experiences into your life by changing your attention. A feeling of gratitude has a high vibration and radiates good energy. Sincere expressions of thankfulness can help you connect with higher-frequency energies in the cosmos because they raise your emotional vibrations. This may result in a vibrational match with advantageous situations, chances, and manifestations that vibrate at a similar frequency. Positive sensations and emotions are amplified by gratitude. Sincere gratitude can have a beneficial impact on your thoughts, feelings, and behavior because it fills you with joy, appreciation, and love. More great encounters may come your way as a result of this positive energy acting like a magnet. You can develop an optimistic and prosperous mindset by being grateful. You may train your mind to concentrate on the positive elements of life and to adopt an attitude of appreciation and thanks by consistently practicing gratitude. The Law of Attraction may work in your favor if you adopt this optimistic outlook. Your visualization technique can benefit from gratitude. When you visualize your goals with a grateful heart, you add positive feelings and energy to your visualizations. As a result, your visualizations may be stronger and more successful in helping you attract the things you want into your life.

Gratitude for the desires

Now that you know that gratitude, when used scientifically, helps you in achieving your desires, I'm sure you are getting curious about how it brings a positive impact on your relationships, happiness, financial condition, physical and mental health. Trust me, as I write this chapter, I'm even more eager to share this information with you. Let's examine some of our most significant goals in life one at a time, and how we can achieve them with gratitude.

Relationships:

Strengthening and deepening existing relationships

A strong relationship is a deep connection between people who are genuinely concerned for each other's emotional and physical well-being. This relationship could be with your spouse, parents, children, friends, co-workers, or boss. People in strong relationship are willing to work through problems together because they feel respected and accepted for who they are. To keep the relationship strong and rewarding, they put each other's needs and wants first and are prepared to make concessions. It's crucial to understand that having a strong relationship does not preclude arguments or conflicts. Instead, it indicates that despite their differences and conflicts, they are prepared to talk to one another in an honest and respectful manner and work to find a resolution that benefits them both. Overall, a strong relationship demands work and dedication from both sides, but when both are ready to put in the effort, it can be tremendously gratifying and enjoyable.

Expressing gratitude towards others can strengthen our relationships. When we acknowledge and appreciate the efforts, kindness, and support of others, it fosters a sense of connection and deepens our relationships with them. Gratitude promotes prosocial behavior, encouraging acts of kindness and generosity towards others.

By encouraging intimacy and openness in relationships, gratitude can strengthen the emotional bond between partners. By expressing thankfulness to someone, you express your admiration for their deeds or character traits, which can foster an emotional bond and mutual understanding. Relationships may develop a deeper emotional bond as a result.

A person may feel inspired to express gratitude to you in return if you show them your appreciation. This cycle of appreciation can produce a positive feedback loop that deepens interpersonal connections.

Healing broken relationships

A broken relationship can be very hurtful, and it could be a challenging experience for everyone. When a relationship ends, It can lead to a great deal of emotional suffering, such as depression, irate, frustration, and lonely sentiments.

Depending on the type of relationship, how long it lasted, and how much the parties involved invested in it, the degree of hurt will vary. It can also be challenging to let go and move on when we have happy memories with them. We often recall back vacations and holidays to commonplace activities like eating together or relaxing on the couch to watch a movie. The broken relationship becomes even more devastating when it is with your intimate partner. Any relationship needs to have a certain level of emotional and physical intimacy, and losing that connection can be challenging. Sometimes, there are little things that are humorous or special to just you and your partner. Those personal jokes may seem meaningless after the relationship is over. When you're in a relationship, you get used to your partner's routines and habits. When that comfort is gone, it could leave you feeling empty. Additionally, when a relationship ends, it can be missed just to have someone to talk to. It can be hard to give up your hopes and aspirations if you and your partner have future plans. Although no union is perfect, there will always be times in your life that you'll cherish. When a relationship ends, those happy times are often the ones that are most easily missed.

I'm sure many of you have been trying to heal your relationship but haven't found success yet. It can be frustrating when we put effort by trying all our ways and don't see the results we're hoping for. Many times, you try to get in touch by calling and texting repeatedly, crying, and nagging in the hopes that they will understand you and eventually call you back. You make every effort to attract attention by updating your life stories on social media and even attempting to make them envious. But let me tell you, you won't get your love back by acting in that way. After a breakup, your ex may feel suffocated and overburdened if you continue to call and text them. They might require some time and space to analyze their feelings and end the connection. You might be keeping them from missing you and calling you if you keep in touch with them. You are also sending the message that you don't respect their wishes or feelings if you chase after them while disregarding their boundaries. This can create a negative perception of you in their mind and may ultimately push them away you can stop them from missing you and calling you by keeping in touch with them constantly. Additionally, by following them and disregarding their boundaries, you are implying that you don't value their preferences or feelings. This can give them a bad impression of you and make them want to distance themselves from you.

The first important thing you can do in applying the science of gratitude is to forgive the person. If you can't forgive the person and keep on thinking about what they did wrong, you will never feel thankful towards that person, which in turn will only make your relationship even more worse. Forgiveness is an important skill to develop because it can help mend strained relationships. It is simpler to let go of grudges and resentments when you are thankful for the positive qualities of the relationship or the other person. It enables you to approach the individual with a more forgiving and understanding perspective, which may pave the way for forgiveness and reconciliation. Gratitude can spur on constructive behaviors that can mend a strained bond. Being appreciative of the relationship's positive elements can inspire you to take action toward reconciliation, such as making amends, being kinder, or expressing gratitude. These constructive actions can help mend the connection and advance the healing process.

Negative emotions like resentment, wrath, and hurt are frequently present in broken relationships. Gratitude exercises can assist you in turning your attention away from these unfavorable feelings and toward the good things about the partnership. You can alter your viewpoint and cultivate a more optimistic mindset by recognizing and appreciating the positive aspects of the person or connection. A lack of trust is another common reason for breakups. By recognising and valuing the good things about the other person or the relationship, gratitude can help to restore trust. Recognizing the other person's good intentions and efforts might aid in re-establishing a relationship and lay the groundwork for trust. Additionally, gratitude can improve communication in strained relationships. A spirit of goodwill and openness can be generated by expressing gratitude to the other person for the positive contributions they have made to your life or the relationship. It can promote honest and open communication by fostering a welcoming and secure setting for discussion.

Attracting new relationships

Gratitude helps you not only in strengthening existing relationships or healing broken relationships but it also helps you in attracting new relationships. Even if you are currently not in a relationship, you can be thankful for the potential partner that you are attracting. Start listing down or imagining all the qualities, both external and internal that you would want your future partner to have. You can be as specific as possible. Now start saying "Thank You" to the Universe, God, or higher power for sending this person into your life like you already have them. Also, thank them for choosing you and loving you.

Make it a routine to **express gratitude** for at least three things each day that have to do with relationships. It could be traits you look for in a partner, fulfilling relationships you've had in the past, or even facets of connections you hope to have in the future. By focusing on the positive aspects of relationships, you can cultivate a positive mindset and attract more great encounters.

You can express gratitude and appreciation to everyone in your life. Sincere Thanksgiving is a powerful way to build relationships and attract like-minded people. It may be sufficient just to show gratitude for someone's time, kind words, or support. This not only creates a pleasant atmosphere but it also demonstrates how positively you perceive relationships.

Now that you are thankful for everyone in your life and your potential partner. Also, remember to feel thankful for yourself. Love and gratitude for oneself should be practiced. Recognize and appreciate your own value, skills, and qualities. Take care of yourself and accept who you are. When you radiate self-love and gratitude for yourself, you attract individuals who respect and admire you for who you are. Be appreciative of your admirable attributes, including your kind nature.

Do not be trapped in a bitter past experience. Bitter past experiences of relationships often hold us back from having a fulfilling relationship as we tend to assume and relate to every situation. It makes us have negative perceptions about relationships. We often tend to believe that relationships will eventually give us pain, that they will cheat, or that they are with us for some selfish motives. Even though your relationship in the past ended, reflect on the positive aspects and lessons it had. Be grateful for the instruction and growth they gave you. Instead of dwelling on the unfavorable aspects, concentrate on the beneficial lessons discovered and the qualities you aspire to find in future relationships. By altering your perspective, you will undoubtedly attract better relationships in the future.

Health:

Mental Health and Emotional wellbeing

Our general well-being and quality of life depend heavily on our mental health. It is concerned with our mental, emotional, and social health and has an impact on how we act, think, and feel. We can develop strong relationships, handle life's daily stressors, and give back to our communities when we are in good mental health. It assists us in making better decisions, solving problems, and thinking more clearly, enabling us to be more productive at work and in our personal life. It can also help us develop positive relationships with people and enhance our communication skills. It is necessary for our general well-being, including our happiness and sense of fulfillment in life.

On the flip side, poor mental health can contribute to physical health issues like heart disease, high blood pressure, and compromised immune systems. This could be explained by the fact that mental health issues can result in unhealthy habits like substance misuse, poor food, and inactivity, all of which raise the likelihood of physical health issues later on. Chronic stress linked to mental health issues can also lead to bodily inflammation, which can aid in the emergence of a number of physical health issues. Recognizing the connection between mental and physical health and working to preserve both is crucial.

It has been demonstrated that gratitude promotes mental wellness. Regularly expressing thankfulness can help lessen stress, worry, sadness, and negativity because when you are truly thankful, there is no room for negativity. It causes a positive outlook and enhances our general mental health by refocusing our attention from what we lack in our lives to what we currently have. Positive feelings like joy, satisfaction, and happiness are fostered through gratitude. Our mood and emotional health can improve when we give thanks for the good things in our lives and concentrate on them. We can become more resilient by practicing gratitude, which enables us to better handle difficulties and failures. Our perspective can be changed from negative to positive by concentrating on the things for which we are grateful. Even in trying situations, this can give us a greater sense of optimism and hope.

When we actively practice thankfulness, it enables us to concentrate on the good things in our lives and fosters a sense of fulfillment and pleasure, which increases our overall happiness. Gratitude enables us to change our perspective from one of need to one of abundance. It encourages a constructive and upbeat attitude to life and enables us to find the bright side of difficult circumstances. Instead of continuously aiming for more, gratitude fosters a sense of richness and pleasure in the now. Additionally, it has been observed that being grateful increases empathy and lowers stress and anxiety.

Self-improvement and personal progress can be sparked by gratitude. It promotes introspection and self-awareness, assisting us in identifying our advantages and disadvantages. We may develop, change, and improve as people by appreciating the lessons we can gain from both good and bad events.

Physical Health

It has been revealed since ancient times that cultivating appreciation can actually improve one's physical health. Appreciation-building is linked to better immune performance. People who express thankfulness on a regular basis report having fewer physical signs of sickness, such as high blood pressure and sleep difficulties. When we are appreciative, our stress and inflammatory levels decrease, which can be advantageous to our physical health.

In addition, gratitude can help people maintain healthier lifestyles. For example, if we are grateful for our bodies and all that they allow us to do, we may be more motivated to exercise regularly and maintain a healthy weight. If we appreciate the benefits of good nutrition, we may be more likely to choose healthy foods and avoid unhealthy ones. And if we value the importance of sleep, we may be more intentional about creating a restful environment and prioritizing sleep in our daily routines.

If you have not practiced gratitude yet for improving your health condition, you can start now. It's never too late. Right now, think about all parts of your body from the tip of your head to the bottom tip of your toes and say "Thank You." You can touch that part of your body or simply be mindful while feeling thankful. You can say it out loud or say it in your mind. What is more important here is the feeling. If you are saying "Thank You" without actually feeling thankful, it won't have any effect. *The feeling is the Key!*

You can touch your hair and be mindful about how they feel on your skin. Say "Thank You" as your hair makes you feel good about yourself and gives you confidence. You can say "Thank You" for your eyes. Our eyes provide us the ability to observe the world around us, to recognize its beauty, and to easily move through it. We frequently take for granted our capacity to see, but it is a gift that enables us to live life to the fullest. Next, touch your nose and say, "Thank You." Our sense of smell, a crucial aspect of how we perceive the world, is controlled by the nose. Smelling delicious aromas like fresh flowers, delicious cuisine, or perfume can make us happy and enjoy life. By filtering, warming, and moistening the air we breathe in, our nose also helps us in breathing. Additionally, it aids in keeping bacteria and dangerous particles out of our lungs. Our general health and well-being depend on having healthy breathing. Say "Thank You" while you stroke your ears. Your body's essential organ that enables hearing and sound interpretation is your ears. They make it possible for you to interact with people, enjoy music, and be aware of the sounds of nature. You wouldn't hear any of the amazing sounds that surround you if you didn't have ears. Your ears not only assist you with hearing but also with your feeling of balance. Your inner ear is in charge of communicating with your brain in order to keep you balanced and prevent you from losing your balance. Now go to the kitchen in your home and look for a lemon. Cut the lemon and squeeze a few drops of lemon on your tongue. Now close your eyes and taste it while being mindful of its refreshing sour taste. Are you feeling thankful now for your tongue and sense of taste? I'm sure you are. Say "Thank You." Now think back to a time when you used your fingertips to feel various textures, such as the softness of a blanket, the roughness of tree bark, or the smoothness of a polished stone. Most of us have probably also held an ice cube straight out of the freezer. Right now, how do you feel? This practice will no doubt make you appreciate your sense of touch.

With the use of thankfulness, you can end all of your ongoing physical sufferings. Here, the sole treatment for the illness and its severity is appreciation combined with faith. Put your hand on the part of your body that is hurting. Touch your upper back and sincerely express your gratitude if it is there. You can close your eyes and pretend your back is perfect and healthy. Say "Thank You." You may do the same for different areas of your body. Establish a specific time during the day and use that window of time to apply this science each day for at least 21 days. The shortest amount of time in any science mentioned in this book is 21 days because it is believed that your subconscious mind needs at least 21 days to be reprogrammed.

Wealth:

Having gratitude can help you attract prosperity. By expressing your thanks for the prosperity you presently have, you can attract more wealth by generating a positive vibe. Being ungrateful for your current riches or money, on the other hand, generates more lack of money. The universe will ultimately notice that you are not grateful for the prosperity or money you currently possess and stop bestowing it onto you.

Use this science of thankfulness to improve your financial situation. You might begin by setting aside some time each day to express your gratitude for the prosperity and money you already enjoy. Your current financial situation, your possessions, your job, your skills, and whatever else you may have are all examples of resources. Keep your focus on the advantages of your financial situation, no matter how small or significant, and express thanks for them.

Be grateful for the opportunities that come your way, even if they don't appear to be associated with wealth or money. This might be an opportunity to begin a new job, enter a business partnership, make an investment, or seize any other chance that could lead to financial success. Give thanks to God, the cosmos, or your higher power for these opportunities, and use them to advance toward your financial goals.

Suppose say you want to attract some specific amount of money, say Rs 5000. Set an intention that you are attracting that amount within the particular time frame. Now write it down on your journal or a piece of paper in present continuous tense, something like "I am receiving Rs 5000 by 21st June 2025. You don't have to worry about the source. Leave the job to the universe. All you have to do is believe and practice feeling grateful for it, as if it has already materialized. To conjure up the emotion of appreciation for the money you desire to receive, use uplifting mantras and imaginative exercises. This makes it easier for you to expect the best and has the potential to make you more receptive to receiving that money. Similarly, if you want to attract a new job, think about every specific detail about that job. It could be the name of the company, the position you desire to hold, the salary of that position, etc. Now set an intention, believe that you are attracting it and feel gratitude about the new job, feel thankful about the selection in the interview, and feel thankful about your new colleagues.

However, remember that it's crucial to act on your financial goals in addition to cultivating thankfulness. You may keep focused on your goals and give the universe a clear intention by practicing thankfulness. You can also be grateful for the progress you've already accomplished. You may establish a potent formula for attracting wealth and fulfilling your financial goals by fusing appreciation with action.

Things that you can be thankful for

1. **Good Health:** For your good health, you can give thanks to the universe. The sheer fact that you can have a restful sleep at night, a healthy appetite, the ability to perform all of your daily activities, and the lack of illness or injury offers you cause to be grateful since it allows you to live life to the fullest and accomplish your objectives.
2. **Fulfilling relationships:** You can feel grateful for having friends, relatives, and other loved ones who give you support, affection, and company. Be thankful for the family that you have with whom you sit down for meals together.
3. **Basic needs being met:** You can feel thankful for having access to basic necessities like clean water, food, shelter, and clothing.
4. **Opportunities:** By showing gratitude for things like education, work, and personal growth, you may appreciate the changes that have been provided in your life.
5. **Nature and the environment:** Appreciating the beauty of nature, especially the natural environment around you, like mountains, oceans, forests, and wildlife, can inspire a sense of gratitude for the earth you live on.

6. **Acts of kindness:** Receiving acts of kindness, no matter how large or tiny, can make one feel grateful and appreciative of others' generosity.

7. **Personal achievements:** You should be grateful for what you've accomplished. When you achieve your own goals, overcome challenges, and reach milestones, you may feel grateful for your efforts and successes.

8. **Positive experiences:** The joy, laughter, and happiness you encounter in life—whether it be from your pastimes, travels, or special occasions can give you a reason to feel grateful.

9. **Learning opportunities:** You can be grateful for the opportunity to broaden your knowledge and understanding and for the chance to learn and grow via experiences, education, and new points of view.

10. **Acts of generosity:** You may experience or observe generosity, compassion, and selflessness from others, which can make you feel grateful.

Starting the gratitude journey

I have been practicing gratitude as a daily routine for five long years now. Initially, I would find it difficult to think about the things to feel thankful for. But I have maintained consistency by writing them down in my journal every day. Through this practice, gratitude actually became my second nature and I actually started to feel thankful for everything in my life. As soon as I woke up in the morning, I would thank God for giving me sound sleep and protecting me throughout the night, for giving me a comfortable room and a warm bed, for giving me another beautiful morning, for my vision, for my beautiful plants and flowers in the garden and the list goes on. Soon my eyes would be filled with tears that the universe has blessed me with so many things.

If you have not been practicing gratitude lately, starting this journey with a journal can help you. Sit down a few minutes each day to jot down in your journal three things for which you are grateful. They can be big or small, like a kind deed from a friend, a breathtaking sunset, or a delicious meal. Gratitude is to be truly thankful for whatever you have at present. To receive what you want, you have to be thankful for what you already have. An ungrateful heart is a sign to the universe that you don't need much of what you have, and hence they will stop coming back to you. If you have been previously unaware of it, then start your gratitude now. A more positive outlook can be adopted by changing your viewpoint and focusing on the positive aspects of your life. Incorporate gratitude sentiments into your daily activities. It may be a morning or nightly gratitude meditation, a gratitude jar where you write down things you're grateful for and read them later, or simply taking a moment each day to reflect on your blessings. Regular Thanksgiving rituals can cultivate an attitude of gratitude and reinforce a positive outlook.

Express your gratitude to persons in your life who have had a beneficial impact on you for a while. It could be a close friend, a relative, a coworker, or even a complete stranger. You can express gratitude to someone verbally, on the phone, or in writing. This not only makes it possible for you to see and value the good qualities in others, but it also strengthens your relationships and fosters a sense of belonging. Also being mindful in this journey is extremely important. Keep your focus on the present and be aware of your surroundings. Enjoy the taste of your food, take in the splendor of nature, and give your tasks your whole attention. This fosters a greater appreciation for the present moment and life's small joys.

Chapter Summary

- Our mental, emotional, and physical health, as well as our relationships, physical well-being, and overall happiness, can all benefit from the strong emotion of gratitude.
- We can experience the transforming power of gratitude in our lives by incorporating it into our daily routines through activities like gratitude writing, expressing our thankfulness to others, and developing a positive mindset.
- Say "Thank You" to your entire body at this moment, from the top of your head to the tips of your toes.
- Give thanks for the money you have right now in order to attract more of it. When you are not appreciative of the prosperity you now possess, the universe gradually takes it away from you.
- You have plenty of reasons to be grateful, including good health, satisfying relationships, and the ability to take advantage of opportunities, to name a few.
- Although it could be challenging at first, consistency will make appreciation second nature, making you feel grateful for practically everything in your life.

II

Speak Your Desires into Existence

Recently, affirmations have become more widely used as a tool for self-improvement and attracting desires. But what are affirmations exactly, and how do they function?

Affirmations are fundamentally just positive remarks that are repeated frequently with the goal of altering one's life for the better. People can change their mindset and beliefs to align with their intended outcomes by thinking positively and repeating these affirmations. The idea of affirmations is based on manifestation principles, which contend that our ideas and beliefs have the power to shape our reality. Scientific ideas such as the law of attraction, which asserts that like attracts like, and the capacity of the subconscious mind to influence our beliefs and behaviors provide weight to this theory.

This chapter will examine the science of affirmations and manifestation and how it can be applied to enhance our relationships, careers, and other aspects of our lives.

After that, we'll speak about how to create affirmations that work, how to use them, the challenges we have when utilizing them, and how to stop negative self-talk. We'll also see some examples of people in real life who have effectively changed their lives via the use of affirmations.

This chapter will offer helpful tips on how to apply this potent tool to build the life you want, whether you're new to affirmations or a seasoned practitioner.

The Magic of Positive Affirmations

Our health, relationships, and professional success can all be improved with the use of positive affirmations, which are effective tools. Positive sentences that we frequently repeat to ourselves are called affirmations. By doing this, we can alter our attitudes, perceptions, and feelings, which will enable us to better our lives and accomplish our objectives.

The following are some ways that using positive affirmations can make a difference in our lives:

Health: Positive phrases called affirmations can help us change our thinking and beliefs. We may alter our beliefs about our bodies and our capacity for healing by using affirmations that are relevant to our health. This may significantly affect our physical and emotional health.

The ability of health-related affirmations to lessen stress and anxiety is one of its many advantages. Our bodies release cortisol during times of stress or anxiety, which can harm our immune systems and general health. Good affirmations can help us break the cycle of negative thinking that fuels stress and worry by directing our attention to the positive parts of our health.

Affirmations can also help us sleep better, which is another way they can benefit our physical health. Our immune system, digestion, and general health can all suffer from lack of sleep. We may be better able to fall asleep and stay asleep when we use affirmations to concentrate on happy thoughts and feelings, which will likely improve our general health.

Our digestion can benefit from affirmations as well. Our digestive system may not operate as it should when we're worried or anxious, which can cause problems like bloating, gas, and constipation. We can support healthy digestion and lessen these uneasy symptoms by employing affirmations to lessen stress and worry.

As a last benefit, affirmations can help strengthen our immune system. When we have faith in our body's potential to heal, we may be more likely to practise good immune-boosting behaviours like eating a balanced diet, exercising regularly, and getting enough sleep. This can help us stay healthier overall and lower our risk of getting sick.

Relationships: A significant method for enhancing our relationships is using positive affirmations. We can rewire our minds and alter our beliefs about relationships when we repeatedly say affirmations like love, trust, and communication.

Past experiences, cultural standards, and media representations of relationships can frequently have an impact on our views and thoughts about them. Unfortunately, these ideas can occasionally be unfavourable and restricting, resulting in unhealthy routines and relationships.

We can start to shift these unhelpful ideas into empowered ones by including positive affirmations into our daily practise. We can reinforce positive attitudes about our relationships by using affirmations like, *"I entirely trust my partner,"* or *"I communicate effectively with my loved ones."*

These uplifting thoughts can help us draw even more uplifting events into our life. We are more likely to find partners and friends who respect and believe in these same things when we have a positive outlook on the prospect of having happy and satisfying relationships.

Positive affirmations can also assist us in developing greater self-love and self-respect, both of which are necessary for thriving interpersonal relationships. We are more likely to find mates who share our values when we respect and love ourselves.

Career success: A great strategy that can assist us in achieving work success is the use of positive affirmations. Our level of success is greatly influenced by our perceptions of our skills. We may pass up worthwhile possibilities that could aid us in achieving our job goals if we harbor restrictive assumptions about who we are and our capacity for success.

We can rewire our beliefs and mindset to be more supportive of our achievements by employing positive affirmations connected to our job goals. Affirmations like "I am capable of developing a profitable business" or "I attract lucrative possibilities that align with my career goals" can be repeated, for instance, if we wish to become successful entrepreneurs.

We may change our perspective from one of self-doubt and limiting beliefs to one of confidence and opportunity by repeatedly saying positive affirmations. We will be more receptive to new chances and take more risks as we begin to believe in our capacity for success, which can result in career progress and success.

Positive affirmations can also keep us inspired and committed to our objectives when circumstances are tough.

It's simple to get down on ourselves and lose sight of our goals when we experience setbacks or struggles in our careers. Positive affirmations help us stay motivated and determined by helping us remember our strengths.

The link between the law of attraction and affirmations:

According to the theory of the law of attraction, we draw to us what we give our attention to. In other words, our thoughts and emotions have the power to shape our experiences and draw in comparable ones. This implies that we can attract pleasant occurrences into our life if we put our attention on happy thoughts and feelings.

Affirmations are an effective method for harnessing the law of attraction. We may alter our thoughts and emotions and draw more uplifting events into our lives by repeating positive affirmations.

For instance, when we repeat affirmations like "I am worthy of love and success," "I am attracting riches and prosperity," or "I am grateful for all the good in my life," we are putting out positive ideas and feelings into the universe. This can facilitate the manifestation of greater prosperity, gratitude, love, and success in our life.

Crafting Effective Affirmations

Affirmations work best when they are personalized, present tense, and positive in nature, and they must also reflect your desires and beliefs in order to be effective. We will go into greater depth on each of these suggestions in this reply.

It's critical to concentrate on your goals in order to produce affirmations that speak to your ambitions and conform to your beliefs. Spend some time thinking about your aspirations and objectives, and list the particular areas of your life that could use improvement. Relationships, a profession, health, finances, personal development, and spirituality are a few examples of these categories. Create affirmations for each of your emphasis areas as soon as you have determined them. To enhance motivation and confidence in attaining your goals, make sure your affirmations are consistent with your beliefs and values.

Affirmations must be written in the present tense and employ positive language to effectively rewire your subconscious mind and change the way you think. By using the present tense in your affirmations, you are communicating to your mind that the outcome you want already exists and is manifesting in your life. Positive language helps to foster the idea that you deserve to realize your goals. Say, "I am happy in my new role," as opposed to, "I will be happy when I obtain a promotion."

Making your affirmations more specific to your circumstances will increase their effectiveness. Take into account your own circumstances, experiences, and goals while personalizing your affirmations. Expressing "I am financially abundant" is not as effective as saying "I am financially plentiful, and my business is increasing daily." Your affirmation will become more customized and resonate with your particular situation if you add specific details, which will boost its potency.

Ten personalized affirmations for your relationships

1. *I deserve respect and affection in my relationships.*

2. I am able to express my demands and boundaries properly.
3. I draw wholesome, wonderful relationships into my life.
4. I deserve to be loved and supported by a spouse who accepts me as I am.
5. In my relationships, I have faith that I will make wise decisions.
6. I have faith in my capacity to forge a passionate and rewarding relationship.
7. In my interactions, I welcome openness and allow myself to be seen and heard.
8. I choose people who encourage and motivate me to be my best selves.
9. I am open to all expressions of love, both giving and receiving.
10. I'm dedicated to establishing solid, wholesome bonds built on trust and respect.

Ten personalized affirmations for your health

1. I take good care of my body every day and am thankful for it.
2. I fuel my body with nutritious foods that give me energy and heal me.
3. My body is capable of helping me reach all of my health objectives.
4. I place a high value on getting enough sleep and relaxing so that my body can repair itself.
5. I pay attention to my body's cues and act kind and compassionately.
6. My body and mind coexist in perfect balance so that I can keep my health at its best.

7. *I chose pursuits that make my life happy and vibrant.*
8. *I let go of all unfavorable feelings and thoughts that aren't good for me.*
9. *I am deserving of excellent health and gratefully welcome it into my life.*
10. *My main priority are my health and well-being, and I'm dedicated to looking after myself every day. I am deserving of excellent health and gratefully welcome it into my life.*

Ten personalized affirmations for your wealth

1. *I deserve to be prosperous and wealthy in every aspect of my life.*
2. *Money comes to me effortlessly and freely, enabling me to lead a life of abundance.*
3. *I draw advantageous chances for career advancement and financial achievement into my life.*
4. *I am able to build money and financial independence via effort and commitment.*
5. *I'm appreciative of the money and abundance I've already attracted into my life.*
6. *I have faith in my capacity to choose wisely and generate more riches and prosperity.*
7. *I let go of any restricting thoughts or beliefs that prevent me from attracting prosperity and abundance.*
8. *I have earned the right to take pleasure in the rewards of my labour and to lead a secure and comfortable life.*

9. *In terms of understanding wealth and how to bring more of it into my life, I am continuously learning and developing.*
10. *I am surrounded by encouraging and motivating people who encourage me in achieving my financial aspirations.*

ॐ

How to Use Affirmations: Techniques

Affirmations can be incorporated into everyday routines using a variety of methods, but repetition and consistency are crucial to optimizing their efficacy.

Journaling is one method for incorporating affirmations into everyday activity. People can reflect on their ideas and feelings, make resolutions, and monitor their progress by recording affirmations in a diary. Writing affirmations in a journal first thing in the morning or right before bed is a powerful strategy. This sets the mood for the day ahead or offers a sense of closure for the day that has passed and helps to start or end the day on a happy note. As an illustration, a morning affirmation might read, "I am capable of reaching my goals today," while a nighttime affirmation would read, "I am appreciative of the chances and experiences I had today."

Practicing thankfulness is another way to incorporate affirmations into daily life. Focusing on the good things in life and expressing gratitude for them is the practice of gratitude. Affirmations that include appreciation might help people feel better about themselves and think more positively. Making a list of things each day for which you are grateful is an effective approach to put gratitude affirmations into practise. "I am glad for my health, my loved ones, and the possibilities that come my way," for instance, may be an affirmation.

To maximize the benefits of affirmations, practice, repetition, and consistency are essential. Affirmations take root in a person's mental processes and beliefs when they are repeatedly used. This contributes to the development of an optimistic and powerful mindset that can enhance mental and emotional health. Saying affirmations aloud or silently to oneself numerous times each day is an effective technique to include repetition and consistency in your affirmations practice. Before going to bed at night or commencing work in the morning, one can, for instance, say aloud an affirmation such as, "I am deserving of love and respect."

Obstacles in using affirmations

Although affirmations can be a helpful tool for personal development, many people find it difficult to apply them successfully because of typical roadblocks. In this response, we will look at some typical barriers to effective affirmation use as well as solutions. We will also go over ways to deal with self-talk that is unfavorable and self-doubt.

Common Obstacles to Using Affirmations Effectively:

Lack of faith: Lack of faith in affirmations' potency is one of the largest barriers to their effective use. It's unlikely that utilizing affirmations can actually benefit you if you don't genuinely think that they can. Start by familiarising yourself with the science of affirmations and the advantages they can offer if you want to conquer this challenge. There are several books, articles, and online resources that can help you comprehend the importance of constructive self-talk and how it contributes to personal development.

Lack of specificity: Lack of specificity is another frequent barrier to effective affirmation use. Affirmations that are too generic or wide could not strike a chord with you or seem applicable to your situation. To get beyond this barrier, try coming up with affirmations that are tailored to your objectives or areas for development. Try something more particular, like "I am confident in my abilities to speak in public," rather than a general statement like "I am confident."

Inconsistent practice: When it comes to efficiently employing affirmations, consistency is essential. You probably won't experience any significant advantages if you use affirmations just sometimes. Try incorporating affirmations into your everyday routine to get past this issue. Affirmations can be said aloud in the morning, at night, or even while engaging in everyday activities like exercise or meditation.

Negative self-talk: Effective use of affirmations can be significantly hampered by negative self-talk. It can be challenging to formulate confident affirmations that ring true if you're constantly criticising yourself or having second thoughts about your talents. Try to become more conscious of your habitual negative self-talk in order to overcome this challenge. Try to replace any negative self-talk you catch yourself thinking with uplifting affirmations when you notice it happening.

Strategies for Dealing with Negative Self-Talk and Self-Doubt:

Practice mindfulness: The practise of mindfulness is being mindful of your surroundings, thoughts, and feelings at all times. By engaging in mindfulness exercises, you can raise your awareness of your habitual negative self-talk and develop the ability to see it when it happens. Your ability to replace negative ideas with positive affirmations is aided by this understanding.

Question negative thoughts: Try to question your negative thoughts when you notice yourself using them. Ask yourself if they are actually accurate or if there is an alternative, more optimistic perspective on the circumstance. You can start to interrupt the cycle of self-doubt and pessimism by confronting negative beliefs.

Surround yourself with positivity: A wonderful strategy to combat negative self-talk is to surround yourself with positive people and influences. Look for pleasant and encouraging friends, mentors, and co-workers. Additionally, make an effort to expose oneself to inspiring writings, lectures, or other kinds of media.

Use positive affirmations: Finally, utilising positive affirmations can be a highly effective strategy for overcoming doubt and negative self-talk. Make affirmations that highlight your advantages and good traits, and tell yourself these things often. These encouraging statements might gradually change your perspective and assist you in overcoming negative self-talk routines.

ॐ

Success Stories

Michael Phelps - Olympic swimmer Michael Phelps has used affirmations to reduce anxiety and enhance performance. During tournaments, he has utilised mantras like "I am the best" and "I can do this" to help him stay motivated and focused.

Lesson learned: Success depends on having self-confidence. Affirmations can help people improve their performance and accomplish their goals by reinforcing good attitudes and thoughts.

J.K. Rowling - Affirmations have helped best-selling author J.K. Rowling overcome rejection and self-doubt. To assist her stay focused and motivated, she has utilised affirmations like "I will not quit" and "I am a successful author."

Lesson learned: Success requires tenacity and tenacity is the key to success. Affirmations can help people overcome obstacles and accomplish their goals by reinforcing optimistic views and thoughts.

Louise Hay- The well-known author and motivational speaker Louise Hay has assisted countless individuals in transforming their lives via the use of affirmations. She came up with the straightforward affirmation, "I love and accept myself just as I am." This affirmation has been utilized by Louise Hay to assist people in overcoming unfavorable thoughts and feelings of inadequacy.

Lesson learned: To develop personally, one must learn to accept and love oneself. People can cultivate a happier mindset and enhance their overall well-being by practicing self-love and acceptance.

Ratan Tata - Indian entrepreneur and philanthropist Ratan Tata. He overcame his fear of failure by using affirmations, which helped him succeed in his entrepreneurial endeavors.

Lesson Learned: Affirmations can assist people in overcoming their concerns and developing resilience, two qualities necessary for success in any endeavor.

Shiv Khera- Author of "You Can Win" and motivational speaker Shiv Khera. He overcame his negative self-talk and used affirmations to succeed in life.

Lesson Learned: Affirmations can assist people in overcoming their limiting ideas and negative self-talk, which can prevent them from reaching their goals.

Deepika Padukone- Indian actress Deepika Padukone overcame her anxiety and sadness by using affirmations.

Lesson Learned: Affirmations can aid people in overcoming mental health problems and developing emotional resiliency, both of which are necessary for achieving overall wellbeing.

Chapter Summary

- Positive remarks called affirmations can assist people in shifting their thinking and beliefs to support desired outcomes.

- By using uplifting phrases regularly, we can modify the way we think, act, and perceive things, which impacts many areas of our lives, including our relationships, health, and ability to succeed in our careers.

- We can generate more wealth, gratitude, love, and success by repeating affirmations like "I am worthy of love and success" or "I am grateful for all the good in my life."

- Focus on your goals, make them relevant to your situation, and use positive language in the present tense to develop affirmations that are effective for you.
- A positive and powerful attitude can be attained via regular repetition of affirmations through journaling, gratitude, and saying them out loud or to yourself.
- Affirmations can help you overcome problems by being mindful, challenging any negative thoughts that may come to mind, and by surrounding yourself with positive people.

III
Rewriting Your Story

You are the author of your own life, which is like a story. Your life's narrative is shaped by the language you use to describe your experiences and by the ideas you have about who you are and how the world works. But what if you had the ability to change the plot? What if you could imagine a better future using the power of language and imagination?

This is the fundamental idea of scripting, a potent tool for influencing your future. Writing up a thorough, uplifting narrative of the world you want needs scripting. By doing this, you may forge a strong and compelling vision for yourself, connect your thoughts and deeds to your objectives, and pave the way for achievement.

We will examine the art and science of writing your future in this chapter. We will examine the strength of your tale and how it shapes your viewpoints and behavior. We'll look at the scripting process and offer helpful advice and resources for writing strong scripts. We will also look into the science underlying scripting and how it impacts behavior and the brain. Finally, we will go over typical problems and difficulties that may occur while writing a script and offer solutions.

You will have a better idea of the significance of your tale as well as the methods and strategies required to rework it, by the end of this chapter. Scripting can assist you in reaching your objectives, enhancing your interpersonal relationships, or leading a more meaningful existence. Let's start the process of rewriting your past and writing your future now.

Knowing the Strength of Your Story

Your life isn't merely a series of experiences and things that happened. It is a story that affects how you perceive both yourself and the outside world. Your views about yourself, the language you use to describe your experiences, and the tales you tell yourself about the past and the future are all important factors in determining your beliefs and behavior.

The first step to changing your story and building a more meaningful future is realizing its power. The significance of the tales we tell ourselves, the idea of limiting beliefs, and the transforming power of rewriting your story are the topics we will now discuss.

Everyone learns how to tell stories. We begin telling ourselves stories when we are very young. We hear them from others around us, read them in books, and watch them on television. However, the most potent of all are the tales we tell ourselves. They serve as the filter through which we view the outside world and ourselves.

Our thoughts and behaviors can be significantly influenced by the stories we tell ourselves, which can be constructive or destructive. For instance, you are more likely to act in ways that support your ideas if you tell yourself a tale about how inadequate or incapable you are. On the other hand, you are more inclined to take chances and work toward your objectives if you give yourself a story about your skills and prowess.

We all have limiting beliefs—stories we tell ourselves that prevent us from reaching our objectives. They might be challenging to spot and get rid of because they are frequently firmly embedded. For instance, you are less likely to seek chances that need intelligence or critical thinking abilities if you think you are not smart enough to succeed.

Limiting ideas may be derived from prior encounters, societal norms, or cues from those around us. They may be imposed by others or by oneself. Whatever their origin, limiting ideas can keep us constrained in negative behavioral habits.

The good news is that you can change your story and dispel limiting ideas. Your thoughts and actions can be altered by altering the language you choose to describe yourself and your experiences. By rewriting your story, you can develop a new narrative that is consistent with your objectives and principles.

Many people have changed the way their stories are told, and the results have been transformative. For instance, Oprah Winfrey overcame several obstacles while growing up in poverty and refused to let them define her. Instead, she changed the course of her own narrative to one of empowerment and achievement. She now ranks among the world's richest and most powerful individuals.

J.K. Rowling, the writer of the Harry Potter books, experienced rejection and hardship before finding fame.

But she didn't want those failures to define who she was. She revised her account and came up with a tale of fortitude and imagination. She is currently regarded as one of literature's most popular and successful writers.

Scriptwriting: An Art

Writing down your future aspirations and objectives in a way that makes them come to life is known as scripting. It is a strong instrument that can assist you in realizing your goals and manifesting your wishes. Setting intentions, defining your objectives, and utilizing your imagination to paint a precise and lifelike vision of your ideal future are all steps in the screenwriting process.

Finding your desires and establishing your objectives is the first step in scripting. This entails being very clear about your goals and why they matter to you. It's crucial to be precise and specific about your aspirations so that you can visualize what you want to accomplish.

Once your intentions are in place, you can begin scripting. Writing down your future vision in detail while utilizing phrases that arouse powerful feelings and conjure up clear images is required for this. In order to convey a sense of immediacy and actuality, you should write as though your desired result has already occurred.

It's time to begin scripting when you've established your intentions. This entails putting your future goals in writing, using phrases that arouse powerful feelings, and conjuring up clear images in your head. Use the present tense to convey a sense of urgency and reality, and write as though your intended outcome has already occurred.

When scripting, affirmations can be useful as well. Positive comments called affirmations serve to support your attitudes and beliefs. Affirmations that promote your intended outcome and boost your positive thinking should be included in your script.

Focus, dedication, and practice are necessary for effective scripting. To keep your vision current in your mind, it's crucial to create your script and return to it constantly. Along with taking action toward your objectives, use your script as a roadmap to keep you on course.

There are innumerable popular screenplays in a variety of genres and styles, and each one was written in a special way. However, the following are some illustrations of effective scripts and how they were written:

"The Godfather"- Mario Puzo and Francis Ford Coppola wrote the book. The iconic crime drama movie "The Godfather" is hailed as one of the best films of all time. The screenplay adapted from Mario Puzo's novel was co-written by Francis Ford Coppola and Mario Puzo. The primary themes of family, loyalty, and power were heavily emphasized as the two collaborated closely to transform the challenging novel into a doable screenplay. Numerous draughts of the script were made, with Coppola famously penning the final scene the evening before filming began. A masterpiece was the outcome, and it took home three Academy Awards, including Best Picture.

"Good Will Hunting" - Matt Damon and Ben Affleck wrote the script The touching drama "Good Will Hunting" centres on the bond between a disturbed but talented young man and his therapist. Together, Matt Damon and Ben Affleck created the screenplay while attempting to break into the Hollywood elite. They took influence from their own college and Boston-based upbringings. They subsequently changed the initial thriller-style script into a character-driven drama. They eventually sold the script to Miramax after receiving numerous rejections, and

the movie went on to win two Academy Awards, including Best Original Screenplay.

"Breaking Bad" *- Vince Gilligan came up with the critically acclaimed TV show "Breaking Bad" which follows the tale of a high school chemistry teacher who, after learning he has cancer, turns to producing methamphetamine to support his family. Following his reading of an article about a man who had established a meth lab in a suburban home, the show's creator Vince Gilligan came up with the concept. The proposal Gilligan made for the show was first declined by a number of networks. However, AMC picked up the show after the pilot episode was well-produced and tested, and it went on to become a huge success, winning numerous Emmy Awards.*

"The Social Network" *- Author: Aaron Sorkin In the biographical drama film "The Social Network," Mark Zuckerberg and his undergraduate classmates establish Facebook. The script by Aaron Sorkin was adapted from Ben Mezrich's book "The Accidental Billionaires." To write a gripping story, Sorkin concentrated on the themes of friendship, betrayal, and the desire of achievement. He performed in-depth research into the issue by speaking with people who knew Zuckerberg and other important figures. The outcome was a quick-witted, captivating narrative that garnered numerous accolades, including the Academy Award for Best Adapted Screenplay.*

Scripting's underlying science

Our brains are structured to respond to both visual and aural stimuli, according to research. Our brains stimulate the same neural circuits when we picture a situation as if we were actually experiencing it. Our inability to discriminate between genuine and imagined experiences is the reason for this. This means that we can influence our behavior and attitudes by envisioning a good outcome and fooling our brains into thinking that it is likely to happen.

Understanding the power of scripting requires a thorough understanding of both neuroscience and psychology. According to studies, our brains release dopamine, a chemical linked to pleasure and reward, when we picture a favorable conclusion. This dopamine release has the potential to produce a positive feedback loop, enhancing motivation and the drive to accomplish the desired result.

Scripting can also support confidence building and anxiety reduction. Writing down and seeing a successful conclusion gives us a sense of control over the circumstance. This can help to lessen our sense of uncertainty and increase our confidence in our capacity to manage the circumstance.

Scripting's efficacy has been supported by a number of research studies. Using a uniform script for communication during handoffs between medical teams reduced errors and increased patient safety, according to research published in the Journal of the American Medical Association. According to a study that appeared in the Journal of Consulting and Clinical Psychology, Cognitive Behavioral Therapy (CBT) with written scripts was superior to normal CBT for easing anxiety symptoms. According to a study that appeared in the Journal of Educational Psychology, students who used scripted dialogue in their peer tutoring sessions improved their reading comprehension more than those who did not. According to research in the Journal of Marketing Research, call center agents who used scripts customized to each customer's demands received higher customer satisfaction ratings and produced more income. According to research in the Journal of Communication Education, inexperienced public speakers who followed a script during a practice speech delivered a speech that was more organized and logical than those who did not.

₧

Obstacles and Challenges in the Scripting Process

Scripting is a potent tool that can assist you in realizing your dreams and achieving your objectives. However, writing a script can occasionally be difficult, and difficulties can occur. Some of the common difficulties that come along in the process of scripting are.

Absence of Clarity: Absence of clarity is among the most frequent problems people run into when writing scripts. This indicates that you might not be certain of what you want to materialize or the measures you need to take to fulfill your objectives.

Negative inner dialogue: Negative inner dialogue is another common challenge that people have when scripting. This indicates that you can have restricting beliefs or unfavorable thoughts that are preventing you from realizing your goals.

Fear: Another typical barrier that individuals encounter when scripting is fear. Fear of the unknown, fear of failure, or fear of success could all apply here.

Doubt: Doubt is another typical barrier to scripting that people encounter. This indicates that you can mistrust your capacity to realize your goals or your faith in the universe's ability to grant your wishes.

"Now that we are aware of the usual roadblocks and difficulties that may appear during scripting, we can take the following solutions."

Determine Limiting Beliefs and Reframe Them: Finding and reframing limiting beliefs is one of the best methods to get through barriers while scripting. This means that you need to become aware of any unfavourable ideas or beliefs that are restricting you and then transform them into affirmations that are supportive of your goals.

Develop Your Gratitude: Gratitude exercises are another powerful strategy for overcoming challenges when scripting. You boost your vibration and draw more uplifting energy into your life when you concentrate on what you are grateful for.

Visualize Your Success: When scripting, visualisation is a potent tool that can help you get past challenges. When you picture yourself accomplishing your objectives, you forge a potent mental picture that can keep you motivated and focused.

Take Action: Finally, action is necessary to overcome challenges when scripting. By making progress toward your objectives, you gain momentum and self-assurance that your wishes can come true.

The right and effective way of scripting

The scripting method has been employed by many of you to bring about your wishes. You've been writing for days on end, but your efforts have yielded no fruit. This is a result of your improper application of the approach. And you think scripting is useless because you aren't getting any results. If you use the proper scripting techniques described here, your belief will alter, and your manifestation will resume working.

Specify what you want: Be certain of what you want to materialize through the Law of Attraction before you begin scripting. It can be a specific objective, a life shift, or something you want to draw in. Clarify the specifics and picture it in your head.

Choose a format: Choose the script format that you want to utilize. You can do it in the form of a story, a letter to yourself, or a conversation with the universe. Pick a format that feels genuine to you and that you can relate to.

Use uplifting words: Use positive words and concentrate on what you want to manifest when writing your scripts rather than what you don't want. To explain the result you want, use words that are encouraging and empowering. Avoid using negative or doubt-inspiring rhetoric.

Write in the present tense: Write your script as though the intended result has already taken place. If you want to give the impression that you already have what you desire, use present tense verbs like "I am" or "I have."

Add feelings: Feelings play a crucial role in scripting. As you write, experience the feelings connected to the result you want. Think about how you would feel if you had already attained your desired outcome. This raises your frequency and helps the Law of Attraction work.

Gratitude: In your script, express gratitude for manifesting your desired outcome already. Being grateful boosts the good vibrations and brings you into alignment with the vibration of plenty.

Visualize: Consider your ideal reality as you write the script. Put your eyes closed and visualize achieving your goal. This speeds up the manifesting process.

Review and revise: Review and revise your script on a daily basis. As you advance on your manifestation journey, you can update it, add new information, or change the language. Make sure it feels genuine to you and resonates with you.

Take inspired action: Scripting involves more than simply writing; it also entails taking motivated action to achieve your goal. Take measures that are consistent with your script while paying attention to your instincts. Action is a crucial component of the co-creative process of manifestation.

❧

The 555 Technique

The "555" technique is one of the most effective types of scripting that the Law of Attraction community frequently employs to assist people in concentrating on their intention and bringing their desires to pass. It is known as the "555 Technique" since it calls for writing a certain affirmation or intention 55 times over the course of five days. The 555 technique can be practiced in the following ways:

Select your intention or affirmation: Choose an affirmation or intention that expresses your goals in detail. It's crucial to keep it upbeat, brief, and clear. You may say, "I am now delightfully employed in my ideal job," for instance, if you wish to manifest a new career.

Prepare your writing materials: Grab some paper or a notebook and a pen to write with. The best way to connect with your subconscious mind is to handwrite your affirmations.

Write your affirmation 55 times: 55 times in a row, begin writing the affirmation or intention of your choice. Write it carefully, mindfully, and pay attention to the meaning that is behind the words. Every time, say the affirmation word-for-word.

Maintain consistency: Write your assertion 55 times in succession throughout the course of five days. Pick a time and location where you can concentrate without being disturbed. Consistency is key in this practice.

Visualize and feel: Try to picture and feel the outcome as though it has already occurred as you type your affirmation. Create a strong sense of belief and positivism by activating your senses and emotions.

Release attachment: Release any attachment to the result after the five days of writing are through. Let go of any fears or uncertainties and have faith that the universe will deliver you what is in line with your highest good.

Act with inspiration: Affirmations alone won't help you manifest your goals; you also need to take inspired action in that direction. With an optimistic outlook and an open heart, search for possibilities and move toward your goal.

The 369 Technique

This is another effective and most commonly used scripting method. The 369 technique entails making intentions and focusing on them for a predetermined amount of time through repeated affirmations. The Law of Attraction's 369 approach operates as follows:

Pick an intention: Start by deciding on a particular aim or wish that you want to come true. It might be something you wish to achieve, a dream or something you want to draw into your life.

Three times in the morning: Write down your chosen intention or desire three times every morning. Use straightforward verbs in the present tense, as though your purpose has already come to pass. To attract financial prosperity, for instance, you may write something like "I am abundant," "I attract wealth," or "Money comes to me readily and effortlessly." Putting it in writing helps you to stay focused and makes your goals more clear.

Sis times during the day: During the day, when you are free and in a quiet environment, write it down six times again in the same place where you have written three times. Say out loud your intention or desire six times. Speaking it aloud strengthens it your thoughts and energies and helps to articulate and enhance your intention.

Nine times during the night: At night, just before seeping, write down your desires again nine times in the same place. The preferable time for writing at night is 30 minutes before sleeping. However, if you need more than 30 minutes in writing, you can start a little earlier.

Repeat for 21 days: For 21 days in a row, repeat the 369 approaches, writing down your objective or want and then stating it aloud and meditating on it. Because it is believed that it takes the average person 21 days to form a new habit and rewire their subconscious mind, many people believe that the number 21 has a special meaning.

Chapter Summary

- By tricking our minds into thinking that a positive event is likely to occur, scripting can affect our behavior and emotions and create a positive feedback loop.
- Limiting beliefs might prevent us from moving forward, but we can adjust our story and get through challenges by revising it.

- It's crucial to concentrate, be committed, and practice consistently when scripting for it to be effective. To make your ambitions a reality, follow your script as a road map and take action.
- While scripting, be clear about what you want, follow a framework, write it in the present continuous, add sentiments, express thankfulness, envision, go over and rewrite your scripts, then take inspired action.
- To apply the 555 technique, write your desire in the clear, short, and present continuous tense. Write them 55 times each day for 5 continuous days.
- To apply the 369 technique, write your desire 3 time right after waking up in the morning, 6 times in the noon and 9 times just before going to bed. Write them in clear, short and present continuous tense. Practice this for at least 21 days to see the best results.21 days are the minimum time frame to reprogram your subconscious mind.

IV

The Flow of Abundance

The Source of Life and Vitality

An important component of the human body is made up of water. In actuality, water makes up between 60 and 70 percent of the human body. The precise proportion can change depending on age, sex, and body composition, but it often falls within this range. Due to variances in body composition, women often have a lower amount of water in their bodies than men. Adult women have a total body water percentage of approximately 50–55 percent, compared to adult men, who have a total body water percentage of approximately 60–70 percent. Men typically have a bigger muscle mass and a lower body fat percentage compared to women, which accounts for the majority of this difference. Generally speaking, as we age, the percentage of water in our bodies tends to decrease, mostly because of changes in body composition. The proportion of water in a baby's or young child's body is usually between 75 and 78 percent. The amount of water gradually declines as we become older.

Medical diseases can also influence the body's overall water percentage by affecting the water balance in the body. For instance, the kidney is vital in controlling the body's water balance. Dehydration or water retention due to malfunctioning kidneys may cause variations in the overall water percentage. High blood sugar levels in diabetic patients can cause excessive urine and dehydration. The body's overall water content may be impacted by this. Dehydration can result from some drugs, such as diuretics, which increase urine production. Other drugs, such as corticosteroids, can increase the body's water content overall by causing water retention. The body's water balance can be impacted by hormonal imbalances, such as those brought on by thyroid or adrenal gland problems, which can change the body's overall water content.

All aspects of the body, including the blood, tissues, and organs, include water. For instance, the lungs and brain both contain approximately 83 percent water. Even bones are composed of water, which accounts for around 31% of their bulk. Numerous internal processes, including controlling body temperature, delivering nutrition and oxygen to cells, eliminating waste, lubricating joints, and assisting in the protection of organs and tissues, all depend on water. It's crucial to stay hydrated by consuming enough water and other fluids since our body constantly loses water through urine, sweat, and breathing. Depending on variables including age, gender, level of exercise, and climate, different amounts of water are required. Adults should aim to consume at least eight cups (64 ounces) of water each day as a general rule.

Because it is necessary for life, water has an impact on entire ecosystems. It supports both plants and animals, and its absence can result in famine, drought, and other catastrophes. It is a strong force that influences our world in a variety of ways. Its significance cannot be emphasized, and in order to fully utilize it, we must continue to learn about and comprehend its characteristics. Its power is used to create energy. Hydroelectric dams produce power by turning turbines using the force of falling water. This clean, sustainable energy source can be used to power buildings and residences. It has an unmatched capacity to corrode, melt, and change the terrain. One of the unique properties of water is its ability to dissolve many substances. This makes it a powerful solvent, capable of breaking down and transporting nutrients and minerals throughout the natural world. It also means that water can erode rocks, carve canyons, and shape coastlines over time.

Water serves a variety of vital activities in the body, making it necessary for human life. It is essential for maintaining human health and well-being because it makes sweating more likely, which helps to control body temperature by cooling the body down when it gets too warm. The lubricant provided by water enables the joints to move painlessly and easily without generating pain or discomfort. It aids in digestion and prevents constipation by breaking down food in the stomach and intestines. Through urine and perspiration, the body helps to remove waste products and poisons, maintaining its health and proper operation. Balancing the amount of blood in the body and making sure the blood vessels are adequately hydrated aids in blood pressure maintenance. It aids in maintaining the skin's moisture and health, avoiding dryness, irritation, and other skin issues. To avoid dehydration, which can cause lethargy, headaches, and other health issues, it is imperative to consume adequate water.

Using Water to Create the Life You Want

With the power of water, you can create the life that you want to lead. Yes! You are correct. Water is a powerful element that has long been associated with the science of attraction in spiritual and metaphysical concepts. It is one of the most important techniques in the scientific theory of attraction, which claims that anything we focus our thoughts and energies on can enter our lives through a series of controlled processes. Since the dawn of time, millions of people have used this science and reaped its wonderful rewards. If you comprehend the power of water and how it functions, you can attract your marriage, restore your health, and get that dream job. This Science has been used by me in many aspects of my life, and I'm pleased with the outcomes. Let us now explore how this power works.

Water is a powerful element of the intention barrier. It has the capacity to both hold and transport energy while also carrying an intention. When water is infused with positive thoughts, affirmations, or intentions before consumption or use, it is considered that the energy of those ambitions can be assimilated into our being and help us achieve our goals. In addition, it cleans. You must have noticed that a number of spiritual and metaphysical activities frequently use water as a purifying agent. One of Christianity's most important sacraments, baptism, uses water to represent the washing away of sins and the rebirth of the one who receives it in Christ. In the Bible, Jesus himself was baptized by John the Baptist in the Jordan River. In numerous Christian rituals, including during Mass, holy water is utilized as a blessed form of water to bless individuals, things, and locations. In some Christian churches, it is also used to bless oneself as a remembrance of baptism and to ask for protection from evil. In a number of Christian ceremonies and customs, water is used to represent bodily and spiritual cleanliness as well as purification. For instance, water and wine are mingled during the Catholic Church's liturgy to represent how Christ's blood purifies humanity. It is additionally employed for therapeutic purposes in various Christian practices. For instance, there is a story in the Gospel of John about a man who bathed himself in the pool of Bethesda and was then healed by Jesus. If you see in Hinduism, water holds a very important position. Before engaging in any religious ceremony or visiting a temple, one cleanses themselves with water. People also pour water on the statues. This act of pouring holy water over a statue or idol of a deity is referred to as "Abhishekam." It is said to represent the divine flow of energy and life. It is used in many ways to depict the divine since it is seen as a sign of purity, clarity, and peace. Because they believe that doing so will please the gods and win their favor, devotees frequently donate water to gods during prayers and rituals. People frequently take baths in sacred bodies of water like rivers, ponds, and lakes to cleanse themselves. The idols of the deities are submerged in water during festivals like Ganesh Chaturthi as a representation of their return to their original form. In the Muslim religion, too, the significance of water can be found in many ways. Muslims perform a ritual called 'Wudu,' which basically means ablution, where they wash their hands, mouth, nose, face, arms, head, and feet with water before offering the five daily prayers. Since it is a symbol of purity and a means of spiritual purification, Wudu is seen as a crucial element of Islamic devotion. They also have a ritual of washing their entire body with water called 'Ghusl.' This is necessary in some situations, such as after sexual intercourse, menstruation, and childbirth. Additionally, it is done as a part of the burial rites when a person has passed away. Muslims are advised to drink water, viewing it as a blessing from Allah (God). The best beverage in the world, according to the Prophet Muhammad (peace be upon him), is water. When you are thirsty, take sips rather than gulps because doing so causes liver disease." A special type of water known as "Zamzam Water" is found in Mecca, Saudi Arabia, not far from the Kaaba. It is of special significance to Muslims and is regarded as blessed. The spring from which the water runs is supposed to have been built by Allah (God) when Hajar (Hagar), the wife of the Prophet Ibrahim (Abraham), was searching for water for her son Ismael (Ishmael). Zamzam Water is used by Muslims for a variety of purposes, including healing and gaining spiritual advantages.

It is said that we can cleanse ourselves of negative energy, limiting ideas, and emotional baggage that might be impeding our manifestations by using water in rituals like baths, showers, or cleaning ceremonies. Cleaning with water can also assist us in letting go of anything that is no longer beneficial to us, making room for brand-new manifestations. Water is renowned for its flowability and fluidity. It frequently serves as a metaphor for the abundance, flow, and opportunity in life. Our manifestations will flow easily and abundantly into our life if we match our energy with the energy of water, which has the attributes of fluidity and plenty. Water has also been seen to reflect emotions. In various cultures and belief systems, it has been linked to emotions. Our emotions can be reflected in the state of water, which might be peaceful and motionless or turbulent and chaotic. We may use the power of water to aid our manifestation process if we are able to recognize and control our emotions as well as establish inner peace and harmony. Water also represents resilience and flexibility. It has a reputation for being able to adapt and alter through evaporation, condensation, and freezing. We may use this flexibility and resilience as a metaphor for our own capacity to adjust to change and overcome obstacles on the path to manifesting our desires. We can use water as a metaphor to remind ourselves to remain adaptable, open-minded, and tenacious in the pursuit of our goals because it embodies these qualities.

Sipping Your Way to Success: A step by step guide to the "Two-Cup Method"

The Two Cup Method, also known as the Two Glass Method, Dimensional Jumping Method, or Quantum Jumping is a well-liked and frequently employed manifestation technique in achieving desires by shifting an individual's mindset from negative to positive. This science is founded on the idea that there are many parallel worlds or dimensions that makeup reality. By altering our consciousness or energy, we may change our awareness to focus on various realities and bring about the results we want. The technique consists of making a symbolic representation of a desired reality out of two cups of water, the power of intention, and water. The method often entails meditation, affirmations, and visualization.

Here are the detailed yet simple steps of the "Two Cup Method":

Collect all the required types of equipment: To perform this method, you will need two cups, preferably clear glass, water, a watch or clock, sticky notes, a pen, or a pencil. If you do not have clear glass, you may also use plastic, steel, or copper glass. However, clear glasses are utilized in this approach because it makes it possible to clearly see the water and the labels on the cups, which contributes to the technique's emphasis on visual imagery and symbolism. The movement of the water from one cup to the next, which represents the change from your existing reality to your desired world, can be seen clearly thanks to the clear glass. Additionally, it makes it possible for you to easily see the labels on the cups, which aids in reinforcing your intentions and maintaining your attention on your intended result. You can therefore imagine more effectively and achieve your goals by using clear glass.

Find a location: Now that you have gathered all the materials, find yourself in a quiet and comfortable space where you can perform this without any distractions. You have to make sure that no one will come while you are conducting this method else people might be thinking that you have gone crazy and performing some magic spells. This will make you break the momentum. Additionally, this technique calls for your whole attention and presence, which can be challenging if there are outside distractions or disturbances. The effectiveness of the visualizations approach can also be increased by relaxing and entering a meditative state while in a peaceful area.

Relax: After gathering all necessary supplies and locating the ideal location for executing this procedure, choose a quiet area to unwind. You can either sit or lay down. Additionally, you can unwind by taking long breaths and unwinding your entire body. To assist calm your body and mind, you can use methods like progressive muscle relaxation or deep breathing. A relaxation technique called Progressive Muscle Relaxation (PMR) includes gradually tensing and relaxing different muscle groups all over the body. Early in the 20th century, American physician Edmund Jacobson created the method. An individual is led through a number of muscle groups, including the hands, arms, shoulders, neck, face, stomach, and legs, during a PMR session. They are told to tense each muscle group for a couple of seconds, then let the tension go so the muscles may fully relax. The goal of PMR is to aid people in becoming more conscious of their bodies' stress and relaxation responses. Put one hand on your chest and the other on your stomach to help you calm your breathing. Deeply inhale air into your lungs through your nose. Feel your chest lift and your tummy enlarge as you take a breath. You briefly hold your breath. Through your mouth, carefully let all the air out. Feel your chest fall and your tummy expand as you exhale. At least ten times, repeat this breathing exercise while concentrating solely on your breath and putting any racing thoughts to rest. If your thoughts begin to stray, gently refocus them on your breathing. You can alleviate any potential stress and anxiety by doing this.

A timer or clock: Set a timer or put a clock near you. This will make it easier for you to monitor the passing of time. It will enable you to fully concentrate your thoughts and efforts on your desired goal, which will boost your chances of success. In order to provide concentration and intentionality to the visualizing process, the timer or clock is used in this technique. Setting a deadline for the visualization is supposed to help you focus and concentrate your efforts more effectively so that you can manifest your desired result. Additionally, a sense of urgency that is induced by the timer or clock can be useful in inspiring you to take steps toward realizing your objective. Simply put, the timer or clock is a tool to keep you intentional and engaged during the visualizing process.

Label the cups: This step entails writing different sentences on two cups to reflect your current circumstance and your intended result. By identifying the cups, you're helping yourself concentrate your thoughts and energy on the intended result and creating a physical symbol of your goal. You acknowledge and draw attention to your present reality by writing a sentence on the first cup that describes your current circumstance. By doing so, you can make room for positive transformation and let go of any negative feelings or resistance you might be holding toward your present circumstances. You can picture and concentrate on what you want to manifest by writing a sentence on the second cup that depicts the result you wish to achieve. Your chances of seeing your desired result in your life improve if you can connect your thoughts and energy in this way. You can picture and concentrate on what you want to materialize by writing on the second cup a sentence that symbolizes your desired result. By doing this, you may make it more likely that your desired outcome will materialize in your life by helping you to connect your thoughts and energy with it. You can also make your own phrase depending on your own creativity but make sure it's short so that you can affirm and concentrate. Now stick one piece of paper on one cup and the other on the other cup. By doing this, you are ready for the next step.

Fill the cup with water: Fill the "Current Reality" cup with water up to the top, and leave the "Desired Reality" cup empty.

Pouring out emotions: Now, hold the "Current Reality" cup in your hands. Look at the water and put all your emotions inside it. Make an effort to completely engage in the process and experience the feelings that come with it. If it is about health that you are struggling with, think about all the pain and inconvenience associated with it. If it is about a broken relationship, recall back about how your partner has been ignoring you, your calls, and your messages. If the person has blocked, you can think about that. Allow yourself to feel all the emotions. At this point, if your heart is heavy and you feel like crying, allow yourself to do so. A healthy method to let go of tension and emotional distress is to cry. It causes the parasympathetic nervous system to become active, which might make you feel calmer and more at ease. Endorphins, which are organic painkillers that can enhance mood and lessen physical pain, are also released. Sadness, rage, and frustration are common reactions to trying circumstances or events, and it's vital to recognize and express these feelings rather than hold them inside. Negative emotions that are suppressed over time can manifest as long-term mental and physical health issues such as chronic stress, anxiety, and depression. So, it's imperative to allow yourself to pour out all the emotions in this step. Above all, you are doing this so as to feel that you are about to put an end to this and shift it to the desired emotions.

Pour the water: Pour the water from the "Current Reality" cup into the "Desired Reality" cup with complete focus and intention. Imagine the river as a metaphor for the transition from your present reality to your desired reality while you accomplish this. You are telling yourself that your current reality is about to shift and change. You are no longer going to be in a lacking state, you are no longer going to suffer or be in pain. This is a tangible illustration of the change you wish to bring about in that particular area of your life. By doing so, you are metaphorically transferring your current reality into the desired reality by pouring water from one cup into another. You are letting the universe know exactly what you want to attract by doing this.

Set an Intention: Spend a few seconds clearing your mind before concentrating on your purpose. Imagine and experience your ideal reality as though it has already occurred. Send them into the "Desired Reality" cup while keeping this purpose firmly in your mind. Start to imagine yourself in an alternative universe or dimension now. This could be a situation in which you've achieved your goals, possessed a trait you'd like to develop, are in a loving and peaceful relationship, or are in perfect health. Allow yourself to think that the reality you want is already happening to you. Say out loud, "It's Done, It's Done, It's Done." To support your aim for the quantum leap, use encouraging comments or affirmations. You might say something like, "I am experiencing a reality where I am confident and successful in my work," "I am receiving new information and wisdom from parallel worlds," "I have a calm and satisfying relationship," or "I am healthy and affluent," for instance. Allow yourself to remain in this altered state of awareness for a while so that you may thoroughly internalize the experience. As your reality has altered, rejoice and feel good. You can decide to remain in this condition for a short while or for as long feels comfortable to you.

Drink the water: Now take a sip of the water, and drink the whole of it. Drink it thoughtfully from the "Desired Reality" cup as if you were internalizing the vitality and essence of your ideal world. Drinking the water from the "Desired Reality" cup is the representation of the behavior that truly experiences and embraces the desired result. By ingesting the water, you are reinforcing your belief that the new reality has already been attained as well as your commitment to it. By bringing your conscious and subconscious desires into harmony, you can more easily bring about the results you want.

Trust and Let Go: This is the last yet the most important step in the Two Cup Method of attracting desires. After following all the steps, if you are still dwelling on the negative emotions or wondering how it's going to work and when it will come true, all of the efforts you put into this method will just flow away. We build internal resistance when we cling tenaciously to our goals and aspirations, which might obstruct the manifestation process. We are able to let go of this resistance and enable the universe to manifest our preferred reality by letting go of our attachment to the result. We can develop a sense of trust and faith in the manifestation process by letting go. When we become overly focused on a particular result, we run the risk of losing hope or losing patience if it doesn't happen the way we had planned. We can release our desires to the universe and believe that we will be led to the best result for our highest good by letting go. Release any attachment to the result after drinking the water, and have faith that the manifestation process is already in motion. Maintain an open mind to chances, and take creative action to create the reality you desire.

It's important to note that the results of the Two Cup Method may vary from person to person, depending on faith and sincerity. While some people could perceive shifts or changes right away, others might observe more gradual alterations. It's crucial to apply this technique in conjunction with other manifestation techniques or practices that speak to you and to approach it with an optimistic attitude.

Chapter Summary

- Being hydrated is important for numerous biological functions because the human body is primarily made of water. The balance of water in the body can be influenced by a person's age, sex, and health. Adults are advised to drink at least eight cups of water each day.
- All life and ecosystems depend on water. It is essential for human health and has special qualities. It's essential to consume enough water to prevent dehydration and preserve healthy bodily processes.
- Water is a strong element that has been used for millennia in spiritual practises to cleanse, heal, and draw in good energy. We can achieve our objectives by putting good thoughts and intentions into the water.
- We can find inner calm, let go of tension and emotional baggage, and be reminded to pursue our objectives with flexibility by using water.
- Two crystal clear glasses, water, sticky notes, and a pen are needed for this quantum jumping manifestation technique. Mark one cup with your current circumstance and the other with the result you hope to achieve. Pour your emotions into the current cup as you would water. Then, symbolizing the metamorphosis, pour the water into the cup with the desired result.

- Depending on the person's faith and sincerity, the consequences of the Two Cup Method may vary; some people may experience abrupt improvements, while others may experience more gradual ones. To observe the effect quickly, consistently apply the technique while having faith in it.

V

Picture Perfect

You can live your ideal life, bring about good change, and accomplish your goals with the use of the effective technique of visualization. Visualization is the process of utilizing your imagination to conjure up images in your head of the things you wish to manifest in your life. You can use the power of your subconscious mind to manifest your objectives by envisioning what you want to accomplish.

Many accomplished individuals, including sportsmen, businesspeople, and spiritual leaders, have used visualization to attain their goals for ages. The foundation of visualization is the notion that a mind is a strong tool and that you attract into your life what you focus on.

You can visualize your goals for your profession, relationships, health, and personal development, as well as other areas of your life, using this technique. You can train your mind to work toward reaching your desired result and eventually manifest it in your life by continuously imagining it.

In this chapter, we will look at the effectiveness of visualization and how to use it to design the life of your dreams. We'll talk about the science of visualization, its advantages, and the numerous methods and resources you may use to improve your visualization practice. We will also discuss typical difficulties that people run across when practicing visualization and offer advice for overcoming them.

Read on to learn the methods and tactics that can assist you in achieving your objectives if you're prepared to harness the power of imagination and begin living your perfect life.

Understanding the Science of Visualization

"Visualization is a technique that involves forming mental pictures of the goals you have for your life. Though visualization may seem a straightforward idea, science has shown that it has much greater power than it first appears."

According to studies, vision can cause the brain's similar neural networks to become active as real-life events. Your brain develops a mental road map of how to accomplish a given end when you imagine it, which can then motivate you to take action. The "mental rehearsal" effect, which describes this process, contends that the mind cannot tell the difference between a strongly imagined experience and a real one.

Beyond achieving goals, visualization has many other advantages. It has been demonstrated that visualization enhances psychological well-being, lessens stress, and boosts confidence. You can achieve your full potential by using visualization to help you eliminate limiting ideas and worries.

You may rewire your subconscious mind to concentrate on constructive thoughts and beliefs by envisioning the desired results. You can then use this to combat any self-talk, uncertainties, or worries that might impede your progress. You can cultivate a growth mindset by using visualization, in which you view setbacks as chances for development and learning.

The science underlying visualization shows how powerful it is at transforming lives, and there are many advantages to using it. We'll discuss methods and approaches for powerful visualization in part after this to help you reach your objectives and lead the life of your dreams.

Beginning with Visualization

It's time to begin developing your own visualization practice now that you are aware of its effectiveness. There are several crucial measures you can take to position yourself for success, regardless of whether you're new to visualization or an experienced veteran.

1. **Set clear goals and intentions:** It's crucial to have specific intents and goals for what you want to accomplish before starting your visualization practice. What would you like to bring into your life? Where do you wish to put your attention in your life? Be explicit and detailed in your goals and aspirations when you write them down.

2. **Create a Conducive Environment:** Setting up a supportive environment is crucial because practicing visualization calls for focus and concentration. Locate a

peaceful, comfortable area where you won't be bothered. To create a soothing environment, turn down the lights or light a candle. You might also wish to utilize aromatherapy or quiet music to make your visualizing experience more pleasant.

3. **Choose the Right Time and Frequency:** Regular visualization of your goals is necessary for successful manifestation. Pick a time of day when you can devote 10 to 15 minutes to practicing visualization. Many people find that visualizing before going to sleep or first thing in the morning is beneficial. Aim to visualize at least once every day, ideally twice per day, because consistency is crucial.

You may position yourself for success in your visualization exercise by adhering to these easy guidelines. We'll examine methods for powerful visualization in the next part after this to help you make the most of your practice.

Methods for Powerful Visualization

With practice, you can improve your ability to visualize, and you can use a variety of techniques to make your practice more effective. Here are three methods to maximize the benefits of your visualization exercises:

Being specific and clear with your desire is the first crucial step in maximizing the advantages of your visualization practice. Being as precise and detailed as you can while imagining your intended result is crucial. Make a mental image of what you wish to accomplish and visualize that reality already being your reality. Pay attention to the little things, such as what you hear, see, feel, and smell. Your visualization will feel more real and have a higher chance of coming true if it is more detailed.

To get the most out of your visualization exercise, it's crucial to express your objective clearly and in-depth. It's crucial to be as clear and detailed as you can while picturing the result you want. Make a mental image of your desired outcome and visualize yourself having already attained it. Pay attention to the little things, such as what you can see, hear, smell, and feel. It will feel more real and have a higher chance of happening in your life if your visualization is more detailed.

Utilizing visualization aids like vision boards and guided meditations is the third crucial technique. You can use pictures, text, and symbols to construct vision boards, which are visual representations of your aims and desires. Use your vision board as a tool to picture the outcome you want by placing it somewhere you can see it every day. Audio recordings that guide you through a visualization exercise are known as guided meditations. They can be a useful tool for individuals who are just starting out or who want a guided experience.

By incorporating these techniques into your visualization practice, you can enhance the effectiveness of your practice and manifest your desired outcomes more quickly and easily. Remember to be patient and persistent, and trust in the power of your visualization practice to bring your dreams to reality.

Using Vision Boards to Manifest Your Goals

Goals, dreams, and aspirations are represented visually on vision boards. The things a person wishes to accomplish or actualize in their life are generally represented by a collage of pictures, words, and phrases. As a tool for goal-setting and visualization, vision boards are frequently made because they can serve as a constant reminder of one's goals and as a means of clarifying and bringing those goals into reality.

A poster board, cork board, digital platform, or any other material can be used to build a vision board. They can be created by printing out images from the internet, printing out images from magazines or newspapers, or using personal photographs. A vision board's components are carefully chosen to symbolize particular objectives or goals, including those related to one's job, vacation plans, physical fitness, interpersonal connections, and more.

Making a vision board may be a creative and enjoyable exercise that enables people to explore their dreams, make intentions, and envision their future aspirations. People can maintain their motivation and inspiration to take action in the direction of realizing their dreams by periodically examining and focusing on their vision board. While vision boards can be a helpful tool for setting intentions and visualizing goals, it's important to remember that they should be used in conjunction with realistic action steps to move toward those goals in a feasible and attainable way.

Utilizing visualization in various spheres of your life

You can use visualization in a variety of areas of your life to help you accomplish your objectives and bring about the results you want. Here are some examples of how visualization can improve various aspects of your life:

Career Success and Achievement: You have the power to have the career that you want and achieve the success that you desire. Imagine working at your ideal job, doing things you enjoy and are good at. Visualize yourself accomplishing your professional objectives and visualizing yourself receiving praise and recognition for your work. Focus on the satisfying, gratifying, and proud feelings that come with professional achievement. If you want to work in a particular company, you may imagine yourself giving an outstanding interview for a specific position in that company. Imagine that your friends, families, and loved ones are congratulating you for getting the job; imagine yourself getting dressed up for the first day at that job. Imagine yourself laughing and enjoying yourself with your new co-workers. Similar to this, picture every particular aspect of yourself attending your dream college or university in order to gain admission. Do not just imagine; feel everything. Feel content with it and express gratitude to God, the universe, or the higher power as though you already possess it.

Financial Abundance and Prosperity: To have plenty of money and to be successful, imagine having enough money to meet all of your needs and wants, as well as all of your bills, and enjoying a prosperous and abundant life. Visualize yourself making wise financial decisions that result in financial freedom as you imagine obtaining unforeseen income. You might be in a state of "lack" and must be having very little money at present, but you have to think about only abundance and not "lack" so that you can actually materialize the abundance. If you are always anxious and keep on dwelling on negative emotions such as "lack," that you do not have sufficient money to pay your bills or that you are not able to buy the tickets for your travel, the universe is going to give you more situations to be a "lack" state. Therefore, accentuate the wonderful feelings of stability, independence, and tranquility that accompany financial abundance.

Healthy Relationships and Fulfilling Social Life: Imagine yourself surrounded by supporting, caring people who value and respect you for who you are if you want to have good relationships and fulfilling social life. Visualize yourself having meaningful interactions and activities with others who share your interests, and picture yourself having fun and laughing with your loved ones. If you want to attract a romantic partner, picture yourself talking to that person, having a romantic meal by candlelight, spending time together having fun, and having your spouse hold you close while gazing into your eyes and professing gratitude for having you. Pay attention to the pleasant feelings that accompany wholesome relationships, such as love, trust, and connection.

Physical and Emotional Well-Being: Visualize yourself in optimal physical and emotional health, with a body that is strong and energized and a mind that is calm and focused, in order to manifest sound physical health and good emotional well-being. Imagine yourself partaking in wellness-enhancing activities like exercise, meditation, and a balanced diet. Imagine playing your favorite sport, engaging in your favorite kind of tracking, or even going to the market and completing your grocery shopping all on your own without help. Think about the feelings of vigor, clarity, and balance that comes from being in good physical and emotional health.

Visualization difficulties and strategies for overcoming them

While visualization can be a potent tool for realizing your dreams and attracting your desires, it's not always simple to keep up a regular routine. Here are some typical difficulties that people encounter when using visualization, along with suggestions for how to get past them:

Focusing on what you don't want: Focusing on what you don't want rather than what you do want is a typical visualization mistake. When someone wants to manifest their dream job, they frequently start off by visualizing it positively, but as time goes on, they start to focus more on the "what ifs." What if the girl seated next to me, who exudes such confidence, is chosen for the position? Many people fall into the trap of worrying about all the terrible things their spouse could do to them, which destroys their momentum, even when manifesting a new connection or healing a damaged one. Keep in mind that it's crucial to concentrate on your desired outcome's good qualities rather than the drawbacks of your existing circumstance.

Doubts: Another common pitfall in visualization is doubt. It is the lack of belief that holds back your manifestation from coming true. The logical mind dominates often, and you start doubting how it will come true. But you have to remember here that universe does not understand the logic and that it only responds back to how to believe it. Find instances of individuals who had used visualization effectively to help you overcome your doubts or go back to times when you visualized and achieved your goals.

Distractions and Interruptions: Distractions and interruptions during visualization might make it challenging to stay focused on your goal. Create a calm, relaxing space where you can practice uninterrupted to get around this. To help you maintain concentration and ward off distractions, you can also use guided meditations or visualization scripts. The time immediately following waking up in the morning or just before going to bed at night is the greatest time to visualize so that you are not interrupted. You can choose your own time according to your convenience if someone else, such as your spouse or parents, lives with you.

Unmotivated: It can be difficult to stay motivated and consistent in your visualization practice. To get around this, ensure your practice has reasonable intentions and goals, and monitor your development to keep you motivated. To build consistency, you can also construct a regular visualization regimen that includes practicing before going to bed or first thing in the morning.

"Nay Sayers": If you listen to "Nay Sayers" and accept their negative beliefs, you may start to doubt your capacity to realize your dreams. You might find it more difficult to picture a successful outcome as a result of this doubt. Naysayers will always try to persuade you that your objectives are unattainable or unrealistic. You risk losing sight of your vision and ceasing to visualize if you place too much emphasis on their opinions. It is crucial that you maintain your attention on the intended result and resist being swayed by these pessimistic individuals' viewpoints.

You may improve the efficacy of your visualization practice and more quickly and simply create your intended goals by recognizing and overcoming these obstacles. Keep in mind to be persistent and patient, and believe in the ability of visualization to make your goals come true.

Chapter Summary

- Visualization is a powerful technique that can help you achieve your goals by using your imagination to create vivid mental images of your desired outcomes. Consistent practice can train your mind to focus on what you want and ultimately bring it into reality.
- Your brain develops a mental road map of how to accomplish a given end when you imagine it, which can then motivate you to take action.
- To develop an effective visualization practice, set clear goals and intentions, create a conducive environment, and choose the right time and frequency for your practice. Consistency is key.
- To enhance the effectiveness of your visualization practice, be specific and detailed in your visualization, use aids like vision boards and guided meditations, and be patient and persistent.
- Vision boards are a helpful tool for setting intentions and visualizing goals. A poster board, cork board, digital platform, or any other material can be used to build a vision board.
- To manifest your desires, imagine what you want rather than imagining what you don't want to happen.

VI

Mirror, Mirror on the Wall

Our sense of self-worth, level of confidence, and general well-being are all greatly influenced by how we view ourselves. The mirror technique is a straightforward yet effective strategy that can change the way we see ourselves and ultimately result in a happier and more satisfying existence. We'll discuss the mirror technique in this chapter, including what it is, how it functions, and how to start implementing it into your everyday routine.

Our ideas, feelings, and behaviors can all be significantly impacted by how we perceive ourselves, which is an important part of our existence. Self-perception is the process by which you learn about yourself by observing and interpreting your own thoughts, feelings, and behaviors. It involves your self-perception, as well as your character characteristics, skills, and attitudes. Many things, including your experiences, upbringing, culture, and relationships with other people, might affect how you perceive yourself.

As your opinions of yourself influence how you feel about yourself and how you portray yourself to others, it is also directly related to self-esteem and self-image. Your self-perception impacts how confident and self-esteem you feel about yourself. You are more likely to feel good about yourself and have confidence in your talents if you have a favorable self-perception. On the other hand, having a poor opinion of oneself can cause low self-esteem and a lack of confidence. Even your connections with other people might be impacted by how you view yourself. A positive self-perception increases your chances of being content and fulfilled in your relationships. However, a poor view of oneself can cause jealousy, insecurity, and a lack of faith in interpersonal bonds. Your career performance may be impacted by how you view yourself. A positive self-perception increases your chances of being driven, self-assured, and successful in your profession. A negative view of oneself, however, might cause inertia, a lack of drive, and a fear of failure. Your mental health might also be impacted by how you view yourself. Positive self-perception increases the likelihood of having good mental health and being resilient in the face of difficulties. But a poor view of oneself can result in anxiety, sadness, and other mental health problems.

Many people experience self-talk that is unfavorable to them, self-doubt, and low self-esteem, which can prevent them from fulfilling their potential and leading happy lives. When people think negatively about themselves, they could start to feel as though they are not capable, successful, or deserving of happiness. These notions may discourage them from taking chances, experimenting, and working toward their objectives. This could be brought on by a fear of failing, a lack of confidence in their own judgment, or a conviction that taking chances is intrinsically risky. But it's crucial to understand that taking risks is a vital and required component of both personal and professional development. In fact, a lot of great businesspeople and leaders say that they learned from their mistakes and were willing to take risks in order to succeed. People frequently indulge in negative self-talk without even being aware of it. It's common for people to be critical of their own errors, weaknesses, or perceived imperfections. They might say, "I'm so stupid," or "I can never do anything well," for instance. Catastrophic thinking is when someone imagines the worst-case situation and persuades themselves that it will actually happen. They might say, "I'm going to fail this test and never get into college," or "If I make one mistake at work, I'm going to get fired." as examples. People may generalize about their entire lives or personalities based on one unfavorable encounter. For instance, someone can say, "I always screw everything up," or "I'll never be happy." Some people may take things personally and hold themselves responsible for circumstances that are beyond their control. They might claim, "My friend is furious with me because of me," or "My relationship wouldn't be going apart if I was a better partner," for instance. People could neglect the positive parts of a situation and only pay attention to its drawbacks. For instance, they can dismiss the compliments they received from their supervisor and claim, "I didn't get the promotion, so I must not be good enough." Low self-esteem and negative self-talk over time can cause emotions of hopelessness, depression, and anxiety.

You must take action to address negative self-talk and poor self-esteem when you become aware that they are having an impact on your life. You can attain your goals and develop a healthier, more positive connection with yourself by using the Mirror Technique. When you become aware of the effects that negative self-talk and low self-esteem are having on your life, you must take action to remedy them. The Mirror Technique can help you achieve your goals and create a healthier, happier relationship with yourself. The premise of the mirror technique is that our thoughts and beliefs have a significant influence on our emotions and behavior. We may experience anxiety, insecurity, or a sense of unworthiness if we have unfavorable views about ourselves, such as "I'm not good enough" or "I'm not smart enough." It might be challenging to get rid of these unfavorable attitudes because they can become ingrained over time. The foundation of the mirror technique is the notion that our emotions and behavior are significantly influenced by the thoughts and beliefs we have. If we have unfavorable self-beliefs like "I'm not smart enough" or "I'm not good enough," we may experience anxiety, insecurity, or a sense of unworthiness. Over time, these unfavorable views can set in and be challenging to get rid of.

Because of its efficiency and simplicity, the mirror technique has been practiced for centuries in a variety of spiritual traditions and countries. In order to obtain insight or establish a connection with the divine, this practice entails spending much time gazing into a mirror. Many civilizations and spiritual traditions have used the technique for ages, including shamanism, ancient Greek and Roman divination, and many types of meditation. "Catoptromancy" was the term for the use of mirrors in ancient Greek and Roman divination. This practice included reflecting visions of the holy or the future using a concave or convex mirror, frequently made of bronze or polished metal. Mirror divination in ancient Greece was connected to the worship of the goddess Hecate, who was frequently pictured holding a mirror and a torch. The mirror was employed in ceremonies to invoke Hecate and other deities because it was thought to disclose hidden wisdom. Mirrors were also employed for divination in Roman culture, particularly in the practice of haruspicy, which involves reading animal sacrificed entrails. The entrails were reflected in mirrors to provide omens and signs. The art of augury, which entailed interpreting omens and natural signs, also featured the use of mirrors. Mirrors were utilized in this tradition to reflect other natural phenomena, such as cloud motion and bird flight. Mirrors were used to connect with ghosts and ancestors in some shamanic societies and were thought to be gated to other worlds. In order to reach the spirit world and receive communication from the spiritual creatures they encountered, the shaman would look into the mirror and go into a trance condition. Mirrors were utilized as a tool for introspection and self-reflection in various shamanic societies. The shaman would look in the mirror and study their own image, utilising it to delve into their own inner world and gain an understanding of their feelings, ideas, and beliefs. The mirror was viewed as a strong tool in both instances for gaining access to spiritual knowledge and insight. Before engaging in scrying, the shamanic practitioner would often take time for prayer, ritual, or meditation to prepare themselves. They would then interpret the images and symbols they saw in the mirror using their own spiritual insight and guidance from the spirits. A "Loving-kindness meditation" also employs the Mirror Technique. The mirror technique is used in this type of meditation to help practitioners develop feelings of love and compassion for themselves. Practitioners can cultivate a sense of self-love and acceptance by looking in the mirror and repeating wishes such as "May I be joyful" and "May I be free from pain." The mirror technique is occasionally employed in "Zen meditation" to increase self-awareness and mindfulness. Practitioners can learn to separate from their inner conversation and develop a stronger sense of presence by looking in the mirror and examining their thoughts and feelings. The mirror technique is used by those who practice "Chakra Meditation" to aid in visualization and connection with the energy centers. Practitioners can gain a greater understanding of their own energy and how it moves through their bodies by looking in the mirror and focusing on a particular chakra. The Mirror Technique is additionally employed in "Inner Child Meditation." This type of meditation is concerned with addressing old emotional wounds. The mirror technique is used by some practitioners to connect with their inner selves and picture themselves as children. Practitioners can develop self-compassion and healing by looking in the mirror and picturing themselves as children.

Understanding the Mirror Technique

The science of manifestation frequently includes the visualization exercise known as the mirror technique. It entails speaking positive affirmations or statements about the things you wish to create in your life while standing in front of a mirror and staring at yourself. The fundamental premise is that by using a mirror to reflect positive energy back onto yourself, you will be able to better connect your thoughts and feelings with the things you wish to draw into your life. This method's goal is to assist you in reprogramming your subconscious mind with constructive thoughts and self-talk that will aid in the manifestation of your desires and the accomplishment of your objectives. This method is thought to have its origins in prehistoric customs like mirror gazing, a sort of divination practiced by the ancient Greeks.

"The Game of Life and How to Play It," written by Florence Scovel Shinn and published in 1925, is credited with popularizing this method. The mirror technique is outlined in the book by Shinn as a means of overcoming doubt and pessimism. Shinn held the view that our ideas and beliefs shape our reality and that we are capable of altering these aspects of ourselves in order to alter the course of our life. Based on the idea of the Law of Attraction, which holds that we attract into our life what we focus on and believe, Shinn believes that our thoughts and beliefs have the ability to alter our reality. We can attract favorable results and experiences into our life by employing positive affirmations and ideas. According to Shinn, the practice is repeating encouraging phrases or affirmations to oneself while looking in the mirror. The objective is to swap out negative ideas and beliefs with good ones in order to alter one's perspective and, ultimately, reality. The mirror technique has gained popularity as a self-improvement and personal development tool since the publication of this book. The method is frequently used by people to assist them get rid of negative thoughts, boost their confidence, and accomplish their objectives. It has been promoted as a means to boost self-esteem and actualize one's desires by numerous spiritual and self-help experts more recently. Authors like Esther Hicks, Rhonda Byrne, and Deepak Chopra have also emphasized the importance of the Mirror Technique in the manifestation process. The results of the Mirror Technique differ from person to person depending on the faith and

sincerity in performing. Therefore, I encourage the readers to be patient with themselves as they navigate the process of self-discovery and progress and to approach the technique with an open mind.

Mirroring your Best Self

The mirror is an effective instrument for introspection and personal development. We can utilize the mirror to reflect on our inner self in addition to seeing our physical reflection when we look in it. The mirror technique is a straightforward but powerful method of self-improvement that can assist you in becoming the finest version of yourself. Improved self-confidence, promotion of self-acceptance and self-love, improved relationships, increased self-awareness, better communication skills, increased focus, decreased stress, and improved visualization skills, are just a few advantages of this technique.

Your self-confidence and self-esteem can be increased through the mirror technique in a number of ways. It assists you in concentrating on your assets and strong points. You can strengthen your positive thoughts about who you are and your capabilities by repeating encouraging words to yourself. You may be able to stop talking negatively to yourself. Many of us have an inner critic that constantly tells us we're inadequate or doomed to failure. You can question these negative thoughts with the aid of the mirror approach and swap them out for constructive ones. It may improve your energy and attitude. You can feel more upbeat and invigorated throughout the day by generating endorphins through smiling in the mirror, which makes you feel confident.

The Mirror Technique encourages self-love and acceptance of oneself. It aids in enhancing your perception of your body and lessens emotions of guilt or humiliation. You can tell your brain that you are pleased with how you look by staring in the mirror and saying encouraging words to yourself. Instead of continuously criticizing your body, you start to appreciate and accept it as it is. Physical attractiveness, prosperity, and social standing are frequently given a lot of weight in today's culture. If people do not reach certain societal norms, it may cause them to feel inadequate or unworthy. People could experience pressure to fit into a particular body type or size, for instance, which can result in disordered eating patterns and a bad self-image. Advertising and the media are potent instruments that can change how people see themselves and the world. Unfortunately, these sectors frequently push inflated beauty ideals that can harm people's sense of self-worth. Images of models and celebrities that have been airbrushed or digitally altered in the media to make them look flawless have been severely modified. As a result, there is a distorted perception of what is deemed attractive or beautiful, which makes many people feel unattractive or inadequate when they compare themselves to these images. A slender body, pale skin, and symmetrical features are among the physical characteristics that media and advertising frequently promoted as being more attractive than others. This can lead to unreasonable expectations about how individuals should look, which can make those who don't conform feel inadequate and low on their own value. Feelings of inadequacy and low self-worth can also be influenced by the continual barrage of commercials for diets, cosmetic procedures, and beauty items. People are frequently taught to believe that they must alter their appearance in order to conform to these beauty standards, which fosters a culture of body shame and self-hatred. The mirror technique gives us a quick and easy way to concentrate on our own worth and positive attributes, which can be particularly helpful in assisting us in overcoming these difficulties. Additionally, by using this method, you can challenge societal norms and promote a more welcoming and inclusive culture.

The mirror approach is incredibly effective at fostering improved empathy and understanding in your relationships. By employing this method, you can demonstrate to the other person that you are interested in learning about their viewpoint and that you are listening to them. You can clear up any ambiguities and show that you have comprehended their message by summarizing what they have stated in your own words. By promoting sincerity and openness, this strategy aids in the creation of a secure environment for communication. You may foster a supportive environment where the other person feels comfortable sharing their thoughts and feelings by demonstrating your willingness to listen and understand. You can also cultivate a deserving attitude about relationships by looking into the mirror and making affirming words to yourself.

The mirror technique is an effective method for fostering self-awareness and personal development. You may improve your awareness of your body language, facial expressions, and general appearance by taking a good look at yourself in the mirror. You can connect with your inner self and become more conscious of your thoughts and feelings by using this approach to physically and visually express yourself. can aid in locating any negative self-talk or limiting beliefs that might be preventing you from reaching your objectives. You can take steps to reframe these unfavorable ideas and attitudes in order to live a happier and fulfilling life by acknowledging and dealing with them.

The mirror technique is a potent tool that can help you become more conscious of your nonverbal communication as well as your tone of voice and the words you use, which can help you communicate more effectively. Simply imitate the other person's words, tone of voice, and body language to use the mirror technique.

The mirror technique can also help train your brain to focus. When you stare at your reflection in the mirror, your brain is forced to concentrate on a single task for an extended period. This repetition can help strengthen the neural pathways associated with focus and concentration, making it easier for you to maintain your attention in the future.

As a type of meditation, using the mirror technique lowers stress and anxiety levels. Your ability to concentrate on pleasant ideas and feelings can help you feel less stressed and anxious. According to research, regular meditation can improve mental health by easing the symptoms of anxiety and sadness. The mirror technique is a simple and convenient exercise that can be performed in the comfort of your own home, making it a useful tool for anybody wishing to incorporate meditation into their daily routine.

The ability to picture your objectives and ambitions may be enhanced by using visualization techniques while observing yourself in the mirror, according to some studies. Your aspirations become a mental picture in your head as you visualize them. You can see a physical picture of that mental image when you look in the mirror, which might help it feel more concrete and real.

Simple steps for applying the mirror technique to your daily routine

Pick a time and location: It's crucial to choose a precise time and location where you can practice the mirror method consistently. Pick a time when you can be alone, and pick a location where you can easily access a mirror. It might happen right after you wake up in the morning or right before you go to bed at night. To aid you in remembering to do the mirror technique every day, think about adding a reminder to your phone or calendar.

Stand in front of a mirror: Look at yourself in the mirror as you are standing there. Try to calm your body and mind as you stand in front of the mirror. Breathe deeply a few times and make an effort to keep your attention on the here and now. Stay focused on yourself and stay away from outside distractions.

Affirm positive statements: The affirmations you make to yourself in a positive manner give the mirror technique its strength. Make affirmations to yourself that are positive while looking yourself in the eye. Pick phrases that hit home with you and leave you feeling good. Use the present tense wherever possible, such as "I am" rather than "I shall be" or "I wish to be." You can use any affirmation that speaks to you, such as "I am confident," "I am loved," "I am deserving," "I am successful," or "I am lovely." Pronounce each of them out loud, repeating it multiple times, and make an effort to say it with conviction.

Implement visualization: Visualization is a potent tool that can assist you in conjuring up an image in your head of the desired result. See yourself achieving your objectives while you examine yourself in the mirror. Imagine yourself in scenarios where you want to be effective and self-assured. Make a strong mental picture by using all of your senses.

Practice daily: When incorporating the mirror technique into your daily routine, consistency is essential. Make it a routine to use the mirror technique every day, even for a short period of time. You will eventually start to notice the advantages of this practice. Keep in mind that developing self-confidence and self-awareness is a journey and that meaningful improvement requires time and work.

By implementing the mirror technique into your everyday routine, you can start increasing your self-confidence and self-awareness and achieve your desires.

Examples of the mirror technique in action in the real world

The mirror technique is a common tool used by elite athletes to prepare for competitions. They picture themselves hitting the ideal shot or performing the ideal routine. They are able to remain confident and concentrated as a result, which can enhance their performance.

The mirror approach is a popular way for public speakers to hone their remarks. They can assess their tone of voice, body language, and facial emotions by looking in the mirror while speaking to themselves. They can adapt and enhance their delivery thanks to this. The mirror approach is a popular way for public speakers to hone their remarks. They can assess their tone of voice, body language, and facial emotions by looking in the mirror while speaking to themselves. They can adapt and enhance their delivery thanks to this.

The mirror technique is used by actors to perfect their body language and facial emotions. They evaluate their performance while looking in the mirror and make any improvements. This aids in the development of more engaging and realistic personalities. In the beauty industry, the mirror technique is frequently employed to give clients a sense of empowerment and increased confidence. People can learn to value their distinctive features and feel more at ease in their own skin by taking a good look at themselves in the mirror.

The well-known actor and comedian Jim Carrey has likewise changed his life by using the mirror method. He claims that he was anxious and insecure in the past, but that regular reflection helped him change his perspective and become more assured and successful. In order to aid him in visualizing success, he even wrote himself a $10 million check, which he carried in his wallet.

The well-known singer and actress Jennifer Lopez has also discussed the effectiveness of the mirror technique. She claims that she utilizes the mirror to set her intentions for the day and to picture her accomplishment. She has been able to accomplish amazing success in her work and personal life by concentrating on her goals and repeating encouraging statements to herself.

Successful businessman and motivational speaker Ed Mylett has discussed the importance of the mirror approach in his own life. He claims that in the past, he had trouble with confidence and self-doubt, but that through regular reflection, he was able to change his perspective and improve his level of self-assurance and success.

Louise Hay, a well-known author and motivational speaker, overcame her fears and changed her life by using the mirror technique. I deserve love and respect; she would tell herself as she stood in front of the mirror. Louise overcame her negative self-talk through persistent practice and developed into a potent force for good change in the world.

The renowned boxer Muhammad Ali developed his self-confidence and self-belief through the mirror technique. He would declare, "I am the greatest," over and over in front of a mirror until he actually believed it. He overcame his fear of failure through this exercise and went on to become one of the all-time best boxers.

Media tycoon and philanthropist Oprah Winfrey has also changed her life using the mirror technique. She claims that while she had experienced self-doubt and uncertainty, she was able to develop her confidence via regular mirror work and go on to become a prosperous businesswoman and TV personality.

Famous author and speaker Bob Proctor has written extensively about the effectiveness of the mirror technique. He claims that he used to be quite pessimistic and critical of himself, but that regular reflection helped him change his perspective and become more effective. He went so far as to develop a technique called "The Mirror Technique" to aid people in making changes in their life.

Famous actor and singer Will Smith has also honed his confidence and self-belief using the mirror technique. He claims that he had struggled with anxiety and self-doubt, but that by consistently working with mirrors, he was able to get past these obstacles and have amazing success in both his professional and personal lives.

Priyanka Chopra is a well-known Bollywood actress who has also found success in the acting and producing industries on a global scale. She has discussed the value of self-evaluation and encouraging affirmations in her life. Priyanka claims that she often engages in mirror work, which has assisted her in overcoming her fears and boosting her self-confidence.

The Dalai Lama, a spiritual authority and recipient of the Nobel Peace Prize, changed his life by using the mirror method. In his lectures, he has stressed the value of self-examination and self-awareness, and he regularly engages in mirror work. The Dalai Lama thinks that the secret to inner tranquility and human transformation is self-awareness.

Microsoft's CEO, Satya Nadella, has emphasized the value of mindfulness and self-reflection in his leadership approach. He often engages in mirror work and feels that doing so has made him a more compassionate and capable leader.

Author, public speaker, and proponent of complementary medicine and spirituality, Deepak Chopra is well-known. He encourages his followers to employ the mirror technique as a tool for personal development because he has written extensively about its effectiveness. Deepak thinks that by using the mirror technique, people can get rid of their limiting thoughts and realize their full potential.

Chapter Summary

- The mirror technique is a visualization practice that combines positive affirmations while looking at oneself in a mirror, aiming at reprogramming the subconscious mind to manifest desires and achieve goals.

- This technique is a powerful tool for self-improvement, promoting self-confidence, self-acceptance, self-awareness, better communication skills, decreased stress, and improved visualization skills.
- It can also be used as a form of meditation to relieve tension and anxiety as well as for focus and concentration.
- Choose a specific time and place to stand in front of a mirror, repeat encouraging words to yourself, and use visualization to picture yourself accomplishing your goals.
- Consistency is key, so make it a daily routine. The mirror technique requires time and effort, but it is a really helpful tool on your journey toward achieving your desires.
- This technique has been used across various industries to improve performance, boost self-confidence, overcome fears and limit thoughts, and achieve personal development. It is now your turn to take the benefit of it.

VII

Acting as If

Do you know what the "acting as if" method is? This effective strategy entails acting as if you've already accomplished your goal, even if you haven't. By doing this, you can alter your thoughts, feelings, and actions, which will enable you to achieve your goals.

The fundamental tenet of this method is that the mind and body are intertwined. You can construct a different reality in your head by altering your conduct and acting as though you have already attained your desired objective. This can aid in overcoming limiting thoughts, boosting motivation, and attracting favorable results.

For instance, you may appear as though you already have a successful business if you wish to establish one. This can entail dressing up like a business person, connecting with other business owners, and promoting your company as though it were already established. You may change your mentality and behavior to become more like a successful entrepreneur by doing this.

The process of making your desires come true through your ideas, beliefs, and deeds is known as manifestation.

The "acting as if" strategy is an effective tool for manifesting since it enables you to match your ideas, beliefs, and behavior with the desired result.

You can send a strong signal to the universe that you are open to receiving what you want by acting as though you have already obtained your desired result. This can assist you in attracting the people, assets, and chances needed to realize your goals.

The "acting as if" technique is effective for several reasons:

You can get rid of the limiting ideas that might be preventing you from reaching your goals by acting as though you have already attained your desired result. You are effectively persuading yourself that you can accomplish your goals when you act as though you have already obtained your desired outcome. This can assist you with reframing your ideas and opinions in a way that is more encouraging and empowering. Let's take the example of someone who wants to be a successful writer but holds the limiting notion that they are not a good writer. You can start to change your thinking away from this restricting idea by conducting yourself as though you have already accomplished your objective of becoming a successful writer. You can start writing every day, go to conferences and workshops devoted to the subject, meet other writers, and talk about your writing as though it has already achieved success. The limiting belief that you are not good enough can be overcome if you start to picture yourself as a successful writer.

You can change your self-image by using the "acting as if" strategy. You are effectively remaking yourself when you behave as though you have already achieved your intended result. You can overcome limiting ideas with the aid of this new self-perception and develop into the person you must be to reach your objectives.

Your motivation and drive to reach your objective can be considerably increased by acting as though you have already attained your desired outcome. You are more likely to feel confident and inspired to take steps to make your goal a reality if you think you have already accomplished it.

You may get rid of procrastination and indecision by acting as if. You are more likely to take action in the direction of your objective when you act as though you have already accomplished it. Because you already perceive yourself as having attained your goal, you are more likely to take chances and make decisions.

Your "Acting As If" Plan Creation

The "Acting As If" plan you create can help you achieve your objectives. By acting as though your desired outcome has already been achieved, you can develop the mentality and behaviors required to make that outcome a reality. You must take a number of crucial actions in order to establish a successful "Acting As If" approach.

Clarify your goal: You must be aware of your goals in order to develop an "Acting As If" strategy. Spend some time defining your objective, being as detailed and concrete as you can. If your objective is to succeed as an actress, for instance, you can define success as landing your first professional job within the upcoming year.

Identify the habits and behaviors of someone who has achieved your goal: Consider what it would be like to have already attained your goal as a second step. What routines and actions would you follow? What would your everyday schedule entail? A successful actress, for instance, might invest several hours each day honing their trade, going to auditions, and building relationships with other business leaders.

Make a strategy to adopt those routines and behaviors: Create a strategy to adopt such attributes yourself once you've determined the routines and actions of someone who has attained your goal. This could entail setting aside time each day to improve on your acting technique, going to networking functions, or creating your own audition opportunities.

Use visualization techniques to create a "reality" that supports your desired outcome: In order to create a "reality" that supports your desired objective, supplement the 'act as if" with visualization. Spend some time each day imagining yourself having attained your goal. Allow yourself to really experience the joy of having achieved what you set out to do by imagining how it feels to have succeeded.

Divide your plan into manageable, tiny steps: Finally, divide your plan into manageable chunks that you can implement daily. For instance, if your plan calls for spending many hours each day honing your acting abilities, divide the time into digestible 30-minute chunks. You'll find it easier to reach your goals if you do this because it will keep you motivated and focused.

Monitor your progress: When employing the "acting as if" strategy, monitoring your progress and making changes to your plan are essential steps in obtaining your intended outcome. You can determine what is going well and what needs to be changed to stay on course for your goal by keeping an eye on your progress. You can stay motivated and focused by keeping a journal where you can record your progress. To see how far you've come, you can also read back over your journal. Even using technology is possible. You can monitor your progress with a variety of applications and tools, including habit trackers, goal-setting apps, and productivity tools.

The "Acting As If" Technique in Practice

The following advice will help you use the "Acting As If" method to your daily activities:

Setting goals and identifying the traits, abilities, or behaviors you wish to develop are crucial before you begin "Acting As If" practice. Break down your goals into more manageable daily steps by being detailed and realistic in what you want to accomplish. Consider what aspects of your life you want to improve while reflecting on your overall life goals. Then, divide those broad objectives into precise, doable activities that you can carry out every day. Break down your general objective, such as practicing in front of a mirror every day or joining a public speaking club to gain experience, into smaller steps, for instance, if it is to become a more confident public speaker. It's also crucial to have reasonable expectations and goals. Focus on making slow, steady progress toward your goals instead of trying to change too much at once, which can cause dissatisfaction and fatigue. Remember that the "Acting As If" strategy is a tool that can assist you in developing the mentality and behaviors required to attain your goals rather than a miracle cure.

Consider a person who exemplifies the traits, abilities, or routines you desire to acquire. It might be a fictitious character or a genuine person. Examine their actions, demeanor, and manner of speaking. Take inspiration and direction from them. You may learn how they react to situations and succeed by observing their behavior, body language, and communication style. It's crucial to pick a person who embodies the attributes you want to cultivate when choosing a model. This individual might be a mentor from real life, a well-known person, or even a fictional character. You can decide to model yourself after a self-assured and aggressive friend or a well-known individual, such as Michelle Obama or Ruth Bader Ginsburg if you want to learn how to be more assertive.

Consider yourself to be a positive role model. This is a potent approach that can assist you in adopting their traits, abilities, and routines. You can obtain a better understanding of their perspective and approach to problems by putting yourself in their shoes. Continue to picture yourself as your role model and adopt their principles. Try to embrace their viewpoint and see the world from their point of view. This can assist you in internalizing their traits and assimilating them into your own identity. As you incorporate these qualities into your daily life, you'll discover that they gradually become more automatic and natural. It's time to put your new thinking into action after you've acquired your role model's attitude. Start by implementing simple routines or activities that support your objectives. For instance, practice standing up straight, making eye contact, and speaking out in meetings if you want to appear more confident. Create a daily schedule and follow it if you want to be more disciplined.

It's crucial to monitor your development and recognize your accomplishments. To keep track of your everyday activities and think back on your accomplishments and difficulties, use a notebook or habit tracker. This will encourage you to stick with your plan and stay dedicated to it.

Let's now examine some methods for maintaining your commitment to your plan:

Clarifying your aspirations and improving your chances of success can be done by putting them in writing and developing an action plan. When you put your goals in writing, you transform them from vague concepts into achievable objectives. You can determine the precise actions you must take to accomplish your goals by developing a plan of action. A great strategy to keep on track is to communicate your goals and plan to someone who can hold you accountable. When you tell someone about your objectives, you develop a sense of obligation and responsibility that may inspire you to carry out your plans. This person can be a friend, relative, or co-worker who is encouraging and supportive.

Instead of obsessing over the outcome, focus on the process. A helpful mentality change that can have a big impact on your general performance and well-being is to pay more attention to the process than the outcome. When your attention is just on the ultimate result, you run the risk of feeling anxious, overwhelmed, and eventually burned out. To keep your motivation and momentum going, it's important to enjoy the ride and celebrate the little triumphs along the way.

Success in any sector depends on your ability to listen to criticism and adapt your strategy accordingly. It is crucial to realize that you won't always get things right the first time around and that there will be times when you need to change up your approach to reach your objectives. Actively seeking out feedback is one approach to being receptive to it. Customers, coworkers, and even mentors can provide feedback. It's critical to experiment and try new things, as well as get feedback. You can find new possibilities and broaden your skill set by trying new activities. Additionally, take good care of your physical and mental health. Get enough rest, move around frequently, eat healthily, and take breaks as necessary. You'll feel more energized and concentrated as a result.

Obstacles in "Act As If" and Ways of overcoming it

This method may be effective, but there are some challenges that may make it challenging to use. We will discuss these challenges and solutions in our response.

Obstacle 1: Lack of faith

Lack of faith is one of the main challenges in "Act As If." It cannot be easy to act as though one has already accomplished one's desired goal when one does not feel one can do so. This lack of faith can appear in several ways, such as self-doubt, failure dread, or poor perception of oneself.

Ways to overcome this obstacle:

Recognise your strengths: Consider your strengths rather than your faults. Recognize your strengths and frequently remind yourself of your accomplishments in the past. Your self-assurance and confidence may increase as a result.

Visualize success: Visualization is a potent tool that can boost your self-confidence. Imagine reaching your goal and describe how it feels in your mind. This might boost your confidence and help you visualize achievement.

Use affirmations: *Positive phrases called affirmations can help you change your perspective and strengthen your self-belief. Every day, tell yourself things like, "I am successful," "I am confident," and "I am capable of attaining my goals."*

Obstacle 2: Fear of appearing foolish

Fear of appearing foolish is another barrier in "Act As If." People may have self-consciousness or anxiety about what other people may think when they act as though they have attained their desired objective.

Ways to overcome this obstacle:

Focus on your goal: *Remind yourself of your objective and the reasons it matters to you. You are less prone to worry about what other people think when you are focused on your objective.*

Practice in private: *If you're uncomfortable, practise "Act As If" alone. Before using the technique in public, this can help you gain confidence and become accustomed to it.*

Change your mindset: *Change your perspective so that you are more curious and open to experimentation rather than worrying about appearing silly. Act As If should be approached as an experiment to determine what works and what doesn't. You may become less self-conscious and more open-minded as a result.*

Obstacle 3: Absence of consistency

When it comes to "Act As If," consistency is crucial. People are less likely to experience the outcomes they want if they just sometimes act as though they have attained their aim.

Ways to overcome this obstacle:

Set reminders: *Set up reminders all day long to present yourself as having completed your goal. You can develop the "Act As If" habit and maintain consistency by doing this.*

Practice regularly: *Regularly, even for a short while each day, practice "Act As If." You may develop the habit and make it* *simpler to adopt by practicing consistently.*

Hold yourself accountable: *Hold yourself responsible for frequently engaging in "Act As If." This can be achieved by keeping a journal, monitoring your development, or finding an accountability partner.*

Chapter Summary

- The "acting as if" method involves behaving as though you've already achieved your goal, which can help you manifest your desired outcome and attract opportunities to achieve it.
- Acting as if you have already achieved your goal can help you overcome limiting beliefs, change your self-image, and increase motivation to take inspired action towards your objectives.
- To achieve your goals with the "Acting As If" plan, clarify your goal, identify behaviors of someone who achieved it, create a plan to adopt them, use visualization techniques, divide your plan into manageable steps, monitor your progress, and make changes if needed.
- The "Acting As If" method can help you develop new traits, abilities, or behaviors by breaking down your goals into manageable daily steps and adopting a positive role model's perspective.
- Putting your goals in writing and developing an action plan can improve your chances of success. Focus on the process instead of obsessing over the outcome, listen to feedback, and take care of your physical and mental health. Communicating your goals to someone who can hold you accountable can also be helpful.
- Acting "as if" you have achieved your goal can be challenging due to lack of faith, fear of appearing foolish, and absence of consistency. To overcome these

obstacles, recognize your strengths, visualize success, use affirmations, focus on your goal, practice in private, change your mindset, set reminders, practice regularly, and hold yourself accountable.

VIII

Ho'oponopono

Long used by Hawaii's natives as a form of healing, ho'oponopono is a traditional Hawaiian healing art. 'Making things right' is the literal translation of the word "Ho'oponopono," which captures the aim of this practice, which is to re-establish harmony and balance both inside oneself and in interpersonal interactions. This art consists of four common phrases. They are-

*"**I'm sorry**": This expression is used to show regret and take ownership of one's behavior or the current circumstance.*

*"**Please forgive me**": This expression is used to request others' forgiveness and to signify a desire to make things right.*

*"**Thank you**": This expression is used to show appreciation for the chance to make amends and mend fences.*

*"**I love you**": This expression conveys love and compassion for oneself and others while acknowledging our shared connection to and*

participation in the same divine energy."

Ho'oponopono's history and roots can be traced back to the prehistoric Hawaiians who coexisted peacefully with the land and water. They held that harmony and balance were crucial for preserving health because they believed that everything in nature was interconnected.

This art was originally utilized in Hawaiian culture to settle disputes within families or communities. It served as a means of resolving disputes, mending emotional damage, and fostering peace. A revered elderly or spiritual leader would normally assist with the exercise and direct the reconciliation process.

The tenets and ideals of Ho'oponopono are founded on the Hawaiian concept of "Pono," which stands for righteousness, balance, and harmony. The emphasis of the practice is on accepting accountability for one's deeds, thoughts, and feelings, as well as seeking others' pardon and reconciliation.

This art also acknowledges the importance of love, gratitude, and forgiveness in mending ties and fostering inner peace. It underlines how crucial it is to let go of unfavorable feelings and thoughts and replace them with constructive ones.

In the modern era, Ho'oponopono has become well-known outside of Hawaii as a potent instrument for spiritual development, healing, and personal progress. It has been modified for use in a variety of settings, such as therapy, coaching, and self-help.

It is crucial to understand the significance of Ho'oponopono in Hawaiian culture and its applicability today, despite the fact that it is gaining in popularity. The preservation of many indigenous tribes' cultural practices and values is a constant struggle. It is our duty as non-native practitioners to respect and honor the cultural roots of ho'oponopono and look for ways to learn from native groups.

Understanding the Four Fundamental Ideas of Ho'oponopono

These four ideas—repentance, forgiveness, gratitude, and love—are at the core of this practice. Each of these ideas is essential to the Ho'oponopono process, and when combined, they create a potent instrument for healing and personal development.

Repentance is the first core idea of Ho'oponopono. It requires taking responsibility for our own actions and being conscious of any negative thoughts or behaviors that might be making our life more difficult. Two essential elements of repentance are acknowledging our mistakes and understanding that we have the power to change both our behavior and our surroundings.

The second essential principle of Ho'oponopono is forgiveness. It entails letting go of any bitterness, hurt, or rage we might be harboring. In order to go on with an open heart and free ourselves from the emotional load of the past, we must forgive.

The third fundamental principle of Ho'oponopono is gratitude. It entails developing gratitude for all of life's blessings, no matter how insignificant they may seem. Recognizing and emphasizing the positive aspects of ourselves and our surroundings rather than our difficulties or difficulties with others is the essence of gratitude.

The fourth fundamental principle of Ho'oponopono is love. It entails developing a strong sense of empathy and kinship for both oneself and others. Love is about realizing that we are all interconnected and dependent on one another as a part of a larger whole.

These four key ideas are used in the process of healing and peace-making in the Ho'oponopono practice. Repentance marks the start of the process as we acknowledge any unfavorable feelings or actions that might be impairing our lives. We next move on to forgiving, letting go of any resentment or hurt we might still be harboring. From there, we develop a sense of gratitude for all the blessings in our lives and strengthen our love-based relationships with both ourselves and other people.

"The Ho'oponopono process is often conducted in a group setting, where individuals come together to discuss their problems and work through their issues. However, it can also be practiced on an individual level using techniques such as affirmations, meditation, visualization, or journaling."

Various Ho'oponopono Forms

Ho'oponopono has changed over time and can now take on several shapes according to the circumstance and the need of the parties involved. Ho'oponopono comes in a variety of forms, some of which are:

Family Ho'oponopono: This is Ho'oponopono's customary method, which is often employed to settle disputes between families. Family members get together to talk about the problems and work on forgiving and reuniting.

Group Ho'oponopono: This Ho'oponopono is a dispute resolution that is employed in bigger groupings like communities or corporations. It entails gathering everyone in the group to talk about the problems and try to find a solution.

Self-Ho'oponopono: This is a more modern variation of ho'oponopono that emphasizes self-healing. It entails accepting accountability for one's deeds and thoughts while striving for inner harmony and tranquillity.

⅋

The Benefits of Ho'oponopono

This practice of ho'oponopono has grown in popularity recently not only due to its spiritual significance but also due to the numerous emotional, mental, and physical advantages it offers. We will now explore the advantages of ho'oponopono and how it can improve your life.

Physical Benefits of Ho'oponopono

Ho'oponopono is thought to have a number of physical advantages, including lowering tension and encouraging relaxation. When you engage in Ho'oponopono practice, you are letting go of unfavorable thoughts and feelings, which can ease physical tension. In turn, this can lower blood pressure, enhance sleep quality, and minimize the chance of developing chronic diseases like heart disease.

Ho'oponopono can also be utilized to treat ailments and physical suffering. This method stresses accepting accountability for your deeds and ideas, which might assist you in determining the underlying reason behind your physical discomfort. By doing this, you can let go of unfavorable feelings and thoughts linked to the suffering, which may aid in the process of healing and recovery.

Mental Benefits of Ho'oponopono

Ho'oponopono provides a number of mental advantages that can enhance your general well-being. This exercise stresses the importance of forgiveness and how it can free you from restricting feelings and ideas. Since forgiveness fosters compassion and understanding, it can also help you have better relationships with other people.

Ho'oponopono can also assist you in cultivating a happy outlook on life. By employing this method, you are concentrating on thankfulness and positivity, which can help you change your attitude and draw good things into your life. This can assist you in getting rid of limiting beliefs and negative self-talk, which will boost your self-confidence and self-esteem.

Emotional Benefits of Ho'oponopono

Ho'oponopono is also thought to have a number of emotional advantages. This exercise can assist you in letting go of unfavorable feelings like resentment, fear, and rage, which can enhance your emotional well-being. You can get better happiness and peace in your life by doing this.

Ho'oponopono can also aid in the development of your compassion and empathy for other people. This method places a strong emphasis on accepting responsibility for your deeds and thoughts, which might make it easier for you to relate to and comprehend other people's experiences. As a result, your interpersonal interactions may get better, and your personal and professional lives may become more harmonious.

Application of ho'oponopono for three important areas of life:

Relationships

Ho'oponopono entails admitting that you are accountable for your own behaviors and responses and that you are to blame for any issues that have arisen in the relationship. By accepting responsibility, you can start improving yourself and your own behavioral patterns. Spend some time reflecting on the relationship's advantages and expressing your thanks for them. This may help you see things differently and make the relationship more positive. Release any resentment, hurt, or anger you may be harboring, and extend forgiveness to the other person as well as to yourself. Although it may be challenging, this process is necessary for recovery and forward progress. Affirmations can help you concentrate on the good parts of the relationship, including love, trust, and compassion. The words used in the chapter can be confirmed. To assist you in changing your perspective and improving the relationship, say these affirmations out loud every day while picturing that particular person. You can also meditate to calm your mind and center your attention on your inner self. This can aid in your understanding of both your own and the other person's thoughts and feelings.

Health

In ho'oponopono, you must accept responsibility for your own health and well-being. This implies that you must actively participate in maintaining your health with a healthy diet, regular exercise, and adequate sleep. Spend some time focusing on your body's advantages and expressing your thanks for them. This may aid in altering your viewpoint and enhancing your life's positivity. Get rid of any unfavorable ideas or emotions that you might be harboring concerning your physical appearance or general health. Accept responsibility for any mistakes or bad habits you may have had in the past that may have led to your current health problems. Affirmations can help you concentrate on the good things about your health, such as your vigor, resilience, and strength. Every day, tell yourself these affirmations to help you change your perspective and add more positivity to your life. You should also meditate to clear your mind and lessen anxiety, which will benefit your general health and well-being.

Wealth

Realize that everything in your life, including your financial condition, is up to you. Accept responsibility for your financial situation and stop pointing the finger at others. If you have a strong negative mindset toward money, rewire it by telling yourself over and over again, "I'm sorry," "Please forgive me," "Thank you," and "I love you." You can speak them aloud or in silence. Imagine yourself enjoying financial freedom and a life of prosperity. Imagine yourself appreciating and enjoying your fortune. Develop a spirit of thankfulness for whatever you have, no matter how small or seemingly unimportant it may seem. You can attract more happiness and prosperity into your life by concentrating on the good things. To reinforce the beneficial changes in your thought and attitude toward money and wealth, you should ideally practice these on a regular basis.

Practicing Ho'oponopono as a group

Ho'oponopono has characteristics that can change based on the circumstance and the form being employed. Below are the steps involved in practicing ho'oponopono as a group:

Gathering: Bringing together all parties concerned in the disagreement or issue is the first step in practicing ho'oponopono as a group. Co-workers, family members, or people in the community are examples of this.

Sharing: Once everyone is present, each person is given a chance to express their ideas and feelings regarding the current situation. Ho'oponopono considers this a crucial stage because it enables everyone to be heard and fosters empathy and understanding.

Taking Responsibility: In this step, all parties are urged to accept accountability for their respective roles in the war. This entails admitting fault, expressing regret, and pledging to do better moving forward.

Forgiveness: A core principle of Ho'oponopono is that forgiveness is necessary for re-establishing harmony and balance. This entails asking for forgiveness from people and receiving it from them.

Closure: After both parties have expressed forgiveness, the group can move toward closure. This might entail doing a symbolic act, like sharing a meal or praying as a group.

Practicing Ho'oponopono as an individual

Begin by accepting accountability for your thoughts, deeds, and feelings. Realize that everything in your life, including how you think and feel, is under your control. In Ho'oponopono, there are four mantras that you can recite to assist you in letting go of unfavorable feelings and mending broken relationships. "I'm sorry," "Please forgive me," "Thank you," and "I love you" are among these expressions. When necessary, say these mantras aloud to yourself or to others. Think about the individual, whether it's a relative, friend, or someone else, with whom you wish to mend your relationship. Repeat the four phrases to them in your head as if they were in front of you. Exercise each day: Make Ho'oponopono a regular part of your day. Even if you don't have any particular connections to mend, put it into practice every day. This will assist you in forming the habit of owning up to your thoughts and deeds and asking for forgiveness. Ho'oponopono is not a quick fix, so have patience. To see the benefits, patience and time are required. Be persistent and patient in your work, and have faith that healing will occur.

Techniques for incorporating Ho'oponopono into daily routines and interactions:

It is very crucial to incorporate ho'oponopono into our daily routine to see effective results. Moreover, we become more conscious of any patterns or ingrained behaviors that might be impeding us or stressing us out when we constantly reflect on our thoughts, feelings, and behaviors. We can lessen the detrimental effects of negative thoughts and emotions on our mental and emotional health by practicing forgiveness, gratitude, and love. We may strengthen our ability to relate to one another, communicate effectively, and settle disputes by taking ownership of our own experiences. We can develop a deeper sense of contentment and pleasure by emphasizing the good things in our lives and showing our gratitude for them. We may take more control and initiative in directing our lives and accomplishing our objectives. Here are a few easy ways to integrate ho'oponopono into daily activities and interactions.

Mindful Breathing: Conscious breathing is one of the simplest ways to incorporate Ho'oponopono into your daily routine. Silently repeat the phrase "I'm sorry, please forgive me, thank you, and I love you" after taking a few deep breaths. You can achieve a sense of calm and clarity by doing this straightforward technique to help you let go of unfavorable ideas and feelings.

Daily Gratitude: Gratitude exercises are a powerful way to incorporate Ho'oponopono into your everyday practice. Spend a few minutes every day thinking about the things you have to be thankful for. This can assist in changing your attention from the negative to the positive and fostering a more impartial viewpoint.

Clearing Declarations: using clearing statements to release negative energy and make room for constructive change. Focus on the issue or problem you wish to resolve while saying, "I'm sorry, please forgive me, thank you, I love you." You can either say it aloud or in silence.

Case studies and individual accounts

There are a lot of case studies and individual accounts of people who have healed using Ho'oponopono. There are examples of people who have used this method to treat chronic illnesses like cancer successfully. Others have spoken of profound changes in their mental health, including decreased anxiety and depression.

One such tale concerns *Dr. Ihaleakala Hew Len*. Therapist Dr. Len successfully treated a ward of mentally ill and criminally aggressive patients at Hawaii State Hospital with Ho'oponopono. After reviewing the patient's medical data, he would work on himself by repeating the words "I'm sorry, please forgive me, thank you, I love you" several times to get rid of any unfavorable feelings or ideas he had about the patient. The patients started to get better after a few months, and many of them were discharged from the hospital.

Dr. Len taught Mabel Katz about Ho'oponopono, and she has since utilized it to better her own life and assist others. Mabel Katz is a speaker and author. In her book "The Easiest Way to Live," she recounts her own experience with Ho'oponopono to overcome sadness and addiction. To help people learn how to apply the practice to enhance their lives, she also leads seminars and workshops.

Best-selling author and public speaker *Joe Vitale* has written extensively about his involvement with Ho'oponopono. Dr. Len taught him about the technique, which he has since used to mend his own emotional wounds and enhance his relationships. He also attributes Ho'oponopono to helping him draw success and wealth into his life.

Ho'oponopono has been employed by UK-based therapist *Paul Jackson* to assist his patients in overcoming trauma, anxiety, and other emotional problems. In his book "Ho'oponopono Secrets," he discusses his experiences working with clients, and he also provides training sessions and workshops to show others how to apply the technique.

Hawaiian shaman and spiritual guide *Kahu Abraham Kawai'i* has employed Ho'oponopono to heal both himself and others. He argues that the practice is predicated on the notion that we are all interconnected and that we may help the world's healing by accepting responsibility for our own thoughts and deeds.

German author and spiritual guide *Ulrich E. Duprée* has written extensively about Ho'oponopono. In his book "Ho'oponopono - The Hawaiian Forgiveness Ritual as the Key to Your Life's Fulfillment," he describes how he personally used the technique to mend his relationships, attract wealth, and enhance his health.

In her clinic, *Dr. Aruna Broota*, a renowned psychologist and counselor in India, uses Ho'oponopono to assist her patients in overcoming trauma, anxiety, and other emotional problems. To show others how to apply the practice for healing and personal growth, she has also led workshops and training sessions.

British-Indian author and speaker *Dr. Rangana Rupavi Choudhuri* has written about her experience utilizing Ho'oponopono to treat herself a chronic illness. She has led seminars and training sessions around India, passing on her knowledge of how to use the practice for mental, emotional, and spiritual recovery.

Indian novelist and public speaker *Amit Sodhia* have written about his success utilizing Ho'oponopono to treat sadness and anxiety. He describes his personal path in his book "The Power of Ho'oponopono," and he now offers training sessions and workshops to assist others in utilizing the technique for self-improvement and healing.

Frequently Held Myths About Ho'oponopono

Ho'oponopono has been more well-known recently, yet there are several misunderstandings concerning the practice nonetheless. Here are a few typical examples:

It's exclusive to Hawaiians: Despite having its roots in Hawaii, ho'oponopono can be practiced by anyone, regardless of their cultural heritage.

Ho'oponopono is just about affirming "I'm sorry, please forgive me, thank you, I love you": While the words "I'm sorry, please forgive me, thank you, and I love you" are frequently linked to the practice of ho'oponopono, they are not its only component. Ho'oponopono is a self-reflection, healing, and transformational process that entails accepting accountability for your thoughts, feelings, and deeds, as well as making an effort to mend relationships with others.

Ho'oponopono can be used without addressing the underlying causes of your issues: Another misconception regarding Ho'oponopono is that you can just recite the mantras without tackling the underlying causes of your issues. However, Ho'oponopono is a holistic practise that necessitates a close examination of your attitudes, convictions, and actions in order to pinpoint and treat the underlying causes of your issues.

Ho'oponopono is a religious practice: Despite having Hawaiian cultural roots, ho'oponopono is not a religious practice. Anyone can engage in it as a spiritual activity, regardless of their religion or cultural background.

It's an easy fix: Ho'oponopono is not an easy fix remedy for reconciling differences or mending broken bonds. It takes time, perseverance, and dedication to work toward reconciliation and forgiveness.

Honoring the Ho'oponopono Roots

It is crucial to honor and recognize the cultural roots of the Ho'oponopono practice in order to do it justice. A distinct and lovely way of life, Hawaiian culture is closely entwined with the land, the sea, and the neighborhood. It is a culture that is firmly based on the idea of "Aloha," which is Hawaiian for "love, compassion, and respect for all." This way of life is expressed in the Ho'oponopono practice, which is founded on the ideas of reconciliation, forgiveness, and harmony.

It is crucial that we spend time learning about Hawaiian culture and helping indigenous communities as Ho'oponopono's popularity grows. It is important to understand that Ho'oponopono cannot be appropriated or made into a product. Hawaiian families and communities have practiced it for centuries as a holy tradition.

Investigating the history, language, and customs of the islands is one approach to gaining a better understanding of Hawaiian culture. Books, documentaries, and cultural events are just a few of the materials at our disposal that might aid in our understanding of culture and its importance. Instead of relying entirely on non-indigenous sources, it is critical to seek out and support indigenous voices and perspectives.

Making informed decisions about where we spend our money and whom we support is another approach to supporting indigenous communities. By making purchases from indigenous-owned companies, we may contribute to their economic emancipation and cultural preservation. We can also think about contributing to charities that aid indigenous populations and their causes.

A Hoʻoponopono practice can be better understood and revered if it incorporates cultural appreciation. Making use of Hawaiian words and phrases in our daily practice is one method to do this. This can involve extending a greeting of "Aloha" or expressing thanks by saying "Mahalo." Additionally, we can incorporate traditional Hawaiian music, dance, or artwork into our work or take part in rituals and celebrations.

It's critical to keep in mind that cultural appreciation differs from cultural appropriation. The act of appropriating entails stealing components of a culture without authorization or knowledge and employing them for one's own benefit. Learning about, respecting, and authentically adopting cultural elements into our daily lives are all part of cultural appreciation.

Chapter Summary

- A Hawaiian healing technique known as ho'oponopono places a strong emphasis on reconciliation and equilibrium via responsibility, grace, and love.
- It can be used to boost health by focusing on the positive, to enhance relationships by taking ownership, and to attract riches by maintaining a happy outlook.
- Affirmations, meditation, visualization, and journaling are some of the methods that can be used both individually and in a group context.
- Simple strategies like mindful breathing, daily expressions of appreciation, and clearing declarations can aid in incorporating hoʻoponopono into your daily routine.
- No matter what their cultural background is, anyone can do ho'oponopono.

- It's not a religious practice, and it's also not a quick fix for settling disputes or healing rifts in relationships.

IX

Walking in Faith

*"The saying **"Faith can move mountains, doubt can create one"** is one that I'm sure we've all heard. This is essentially a proverb that emphasizes the strength of faith and the negative consequences of doubt. The expression is frequently used metaphorically to convey the effects of belief and skepticism on our lives and the environment in which we live."*

The underlying message of the proverb is that having confidence in something can give us the courage and determination to face situations that, at first glance, appear insurmountable. We are more likely to take chances and pursue our goals with confidence when we have trust in ourselves, our skills, or a greater power because we believe that we have the strength to go through any challenges that stand in our way.

Contrarily, skepticism might turn into a figurative mountain that is challenging or impossible to climb. We can experience paralysis by dread, indecision, and uneasiness when we doubt ourselves, our capacities, or our convictions. Doubt might prevent us from acting or from pursuing our objectives, which can lead to missed chances and diminished potential.

Although the function of faith is frequently overlooked, specific techniques and practices, such as the law of attraction, visualization, and affirmations, are frequently linked to manifestation. In this context, faith refers to our confidence in the universe, our own abilities, and the power of manifestation.

We will discuss the relationship between manifestation and faith in this chapter, as well as how crucial faith is to reaching our manifestation objectives.

Manifesting and faith are closely related since doing so calls for a strong feeling of faith in the cosmos and our capacity to shape our reality. We are more likely to match our thoughts, feelings, and actions with our desires and take inspired action to realize them when we have faith in both ourselves and the universe.

The law of attraction, a fundamental idea in the manifestation process, is also fundamentally dependent on faith. According to the law of attraction, circumstances and experiences that are in line with our energetic frequency are drawn to us. We may more readily align our energy with our desires and draw them into our reality when we have faith in them and think that they are already on their way to us.

Being able to get through any doubt, fear, or limiting beliefs that may be preventing us from manifesting our goals requires trust. When we have faith in the manifestation process, we can let go of our attachment to the result and have faith that everything is working out as it should.

Faith also enables us to keep a positive outlook and concentrate on what we desire as opposed to what we don't want. We can more readily link our energy with our desires and draw them into our reality by focusing on their good qualities of them and thinking that they are already on their way to us.

Faith may also keep us energized and motivated as we work toward our goals. We are more inclined to take inspired action in the direction of fulfilling our dreams and to persevere in the face of difficulties and challenges when we think that they are possible and achievable.

What is faith?

A deep belief or confidence in something or someone, frequently without justification or evidence, is referred to as having faith. It is a cornerstone of numerous faiths and spiritual traditions and is frequently viewed as the way to realize one's potential.

Different religions and belief systems place a very different emphasis on faith. Christians are urged to have confidence in both the teachings of Jesus Christ and the existence of God, which is frequently viewed as a requirement for salvation. Islam places a high value on faith in Allah, and the Quran stresses the significance of relying on God's guidance and mercy. Hinduism frequently expresses religion via the adoration of many gods and the quest for enlightenment. In Buddhism, the first of the five spiritual faculties is faith (Shraddha). It provides the basis for all other spiritual disciplines and leads to enlightenment and wisdom. Buddhists adhere to the Eightfold Path and the Four Noble Truths. In Judaism, faith

(Emunah) is also significant. Jews uphold the doctrine of the one God and abide by the Torah's teachings. Through prayer, Torah study, and deeds of kindness, faith is demonstrated.

Regardless of the particular belief system, faith is frequently viewed as a potent force that may assist people in achieving their objectives and overcoming challenges. This is so that we can perform actions that are consistent with our beliefs and goals. Faith has the power to influence our thoughts and emotions.

For instance, if a person believes they will find a rewarding profession, they are more likely to take the initiative to look for work and advance their skills. On the other hand, a person may be more likely to give up on their goals or fail to put in the required effort if they lack confidence in their capacity to accomplish.

Faith is frequently viewed in the context of manifestation as being essential to fulfilling one's desires. We may connect our thoughts and emotions with our desired outcome and take inspired action to make it a reality by having faith that what we want is feasible and putting our faith in the universe to bring it to us.

Investigating how faith and manifestation are related

In the manifestation process, faith is essential. Our attitudes and beliefs influence our reality, therefore having faith in our capacity to manifest our wishes can significantly boost the chances of success.

Faith has a significant impact on our thoughts and feelings. When we have faith in something, we are more inclined to concentrate on its advantages and have an upbeat outlook on it. By adopting a positive outlook, we can influence the experiences and results that come into our life.

On the other hand, we can encounter unfavourable ideas and feelings that could obstruct our efforts to realise our wishes if we lack faith in our capacity to do so. Fear, mistrust, and uncertainty can all prevent us from attracting the things we want.

The law of attraction is a well-known method of manifesting that places an emphasis on the influence of our thoughts and emotions in drawing about our wishes. By concentrating on happy ideas and feelings, we can attract more pleasant experiences into our life since, according to the law of attraction, what we focus on increases.

Faith is essential to the law of attraction because it keeps us optimistic and makes us believe that the universe will provide for our needs. We can draw more fulfilling events and outcomes into our life by having faith in our capacity to materialize our desires.

There are numerous instances where faith has assisted people in achieving their goals.

"The case of Olympic athlete Louis Zamperini is one illustration. Zamperini served as a prisoner of war in a Japanese internment camp during World War II. He survived repeated beatings and severe surroundings, yet he never wavered in his trust in God or his conviction that he would one day be free. He even promised God that if he made it through the war, he would live his life in service to others. After his eventual release, Zamperini fulfilled his vow by turning into a motivational speaker and philanthropist.

Another example is the life of well-known Christian author and pastor Joel Osteen. Osteen attributes both his unshakeable faith in God and his conviction in the efficacy of positive thinking for his success. He frequently shares the tale of how he and his wife, Victoria, began their church with just a few members in a modest rental facility, but through their perseverance and faith, it grew to be one of the biggest and most prosperous churches in the country.

Media tycoon Oprah Winfrey is well-known for her work as a talk show host, actress, and producer. Winfrey has publicly discussed how her faith has assisted her in overcoming a variety of obstacles throughout her life, including a challenging childhood and battles with weight and self-esteem. She credits her faith in a higher power and her dedication to leading a life guided by purpose for much of her success.

A motivational speaker and author named Nick Vujicic was born without arms or legs. Despite his physical limitations, Vujicic has achieved professional success and is renowned for his motivational speeches on overcoming hardship and leading a life of meaning. He attributes his ability to overcome his obstacles and achieve his dreams to his trust in God.

As a medic in the American Army, Desmond Doss participated in World War II. During the Battle of Okinawa, Doss valiantly saved the lives of numerous of his fellow soldiers despite being a conscientious objector and refusing to carry a weapon. Doss credited his trust in God and his conviction about the effectiveness of prayer for his bravery and success on the battlefield. Later, "Hacksaw Ridge," a film based on his life, was released in 2016."

These are but a few instances, but there are numerous other people who have employed their faith in order to realize their aspirations and accomplish their objectives. Faith may be a potent tool for assisting people in overcoming challenges and realizing their goals, whether it is through prayer, optimistic thinking, or a belief in a higher power.

🙰

A Guide to Develop Unwavering Faith to Manifest Your Desires

Developing unwavering faith is an important part of the manifestation process. Here are some techniques for boosting your trust and expanding your capacity for wish manifestation:

1. **Developing a positive mindset and beliefs:** Positive thinking and beliefs are essential for developing faith because they enable people to concentrate on possibilities rather than the constraints of a circumstance. It is among the most crucial steps in developing faith. This entails putting more emphasis on the good things in your life as opposed to focusing on the bad. You can achieve this by employing positive affirmations, such as talking to yourself in an empowering manner and concentrating on your accomplishments and abilities. You can increase your confidence in your abilities to manifest your wishes by taking on a positive outlook.

2. **Strengthening your spiritual practice**: Many people's spiritual ideas and practices serve as the foundation for their faith. Developing your spiritual practice can be a highly effective strategy to create faith for manifestation. This can entail frequent meditation, prayer, or other spiritual exercises that support your connection to your inner knowledge and intuition. Even in the face of trying situations, regular prayer and meditation can help you develop a sense of inner peace and tranquility. This can strengthen your faith by allowing you to have more confidence in your higher power's capacity to lead and safeguard you. You can boost your belief in a higher power and your confidence that the universe will grant your wishes by developing your spiritual practice.

3. **Overcoming limiting beliefs and doubts**: Limiting beliefs and uncertainties are among the biggest barriers to developing faith. These ideas that prevent you from achieving your goals could be ones about who you are, what you are capable of, or how the world works. You can use self-reflection and introspection to determine the source of your limiting beliefs in order to dispel them. You can then try to transform these ideas into ones that support your manifestation objectives and are more empowering and uplifting. Find the limiting notion that is preventing you. This could be the idea that you're not talented, intelligent, or competent enough. Your limiting beliefs should be listed in as much detail as you can. Once you've determined what your limiting belief is, challenge it. Consider whether this notion is supported by facts or if it is merely a self-defeating tale. After you've questioned a belief, put it to the test. Find instances of people who have overcome similar ideas

and evidence that refutes the belief. Transform the restrictive belief into a motivating and empowering one. Reframe your limiting thought, for instance, from "I'm not smart enough" to "I have the capacity to learn and improve." Finally, put your new belief into practice.

4. **Practicing gratitude and visualization:** Gratitude and visualization exercises are two other ways to develop your faith. In contrast to visualization, which involves picturing yourself achieving your goals, gratitude involves focusing on the positive aspects of your life and feeling grateful for them. You can boost your confidence in your capacity to manifest your desires and raise your general sense of positivity and optimism by engaging in gratitude and visualization exercises. Spend a few minutes every day thinking about your blessings. This may include having a roof over your head or seeing a loved one smile. Allow yourself to experience the feelings that come with success by visualizing yourself as having already accomplished it. For instance, picture yourself in your new position, happy and pleased, if you seek a promotion at work. You increase your chances of receiving more good things in your life and build your trust by focusing on all the blessings the universe has given you and visualizing the desired result.

Issues with manifestation and faith

Although developing faith is crucial for manifestation, there are a number of obstacles that may prevent us from achieving our goals. The following are some typical challenges and advice for conquering them with faith:

First, manifestation is frequently hampered by anxiety and impatience. Impatience can develop when we become dissatisfied that our desires are not materializing soon enough, while fear can develop when we have doubts about our ability to materialise our desires. It is crucial to have faith in the universe's timetable and trust that events are transpiring as they should in order to overcome these challenges. We can develop a sense of serenity and faith in the process by letting go of our connection to the result and concentrating on the here and now.

Secondly, Self-doubt and restrictive thoughts can sometimes prevent us from achieving our goals. It's possible that we unwittingly prevent ourselves from getting the things we want when we have doubts about our talents or ourselves. It is crucial to engage in self-reflection and introspection to understand the origins of these ideas in order to overcome these challenges. We can then try to transform these beliefs into more empowered ones that help us achieve our manifestation objectives.

Finally, it can be difficult to maintain motivation and concentration on our manifestation goals. When we face failures or challenges, it can be simple to become side-tracked or demoralized. It's crucial to have a sense of purpose and enthusiasm for our goals if we want to stay motivated and focused. This may entail establishing specific objectives, making a vision board or other visual aids, and periodically reminding ourselves of the reasons our goals are significant to us.

Overall, cultivating faith can help us get past these difficulties and accomplish our manifestation objectives, even though there are many obstacles to faith and manifestation. We may design the life we want by having trust in the process, letting go of our connection to the result, and being motivated and focused.

Chapter Summary

- We can overcome obstacles and attain our goals with the support of the mighty force of faith.
- While faith helps you in achieving your goals, doubt hinders your potential.
- In order to match our energy with our desires and bring them about through manifestation, faith is necessary.
- Having faith in our capacity to bring about the desires we have affects our thoughts and feelings, which impact the reality we experience.
- To develop faith for manifestation, focus on positive thinking, strengthen spiritual practices, overcome limiting beliefs, and practice gratitude and visualization. These techniques can help you feel more capable and improve your odds of succeeding in your objectives.
- We can overcome challenges like impatience, self-doubt, and a lack of motivation by believing in the process, changing our limiting beliefs, and remaining committed to our objectives. We can manifest the life we want if we have faith.

X

Action as the Fuel

We've all had a dream, a wish, or a goal that we've wanted to accomplish at some point in our lives. Perhaps it's to launch our own company, write a book, pick up a foreign tongue, or embark on a global journey. It's simple to get fired up about our goals and picture them coming true, but it's quite another to take the essential actions to make them a reality.

The benefits of making proactive efforts toward your goals, the common hazards of inaction and procrastination, the distinction between passive visualization and active manifestation, and why taking action is necessary to manifest your wants are all covered in this chapter. Understanding the value of action can help you map out a clear path to your goals and accomplish them more swiftly and successfully.

The Importance of Taking Action to Manifest Your Desires

The conviction that you have the ability to design the life you want is the cornerstone of manifesting your desires.

To make your wishes come true, though, you need more than just this belief. A crucial component of the process is acting. Your objectives become attainable goals when you take action to make them happen—your transition from wishful thought to practical action as a result. Actions fuel your desires to make it into reality. Without taking any action, your dreams remain just that—wishes you have for the future.

The Distinction Between Active Manifestation and Passive Visualization

The first stage in the manifestation process is to visualize your goals. By visualizing what you desire, you engage your imagination, evoke your emotions, and create the conditions for your subconscious mind to begin advancing your objectives. However, using visualization alone won't help you achieve your goals.

Active manifestation entails making progress toward your objectives in a concrete way. It entails going beyond the stage of visualization and taking the initiative to achieve your goals. This could entail conducting research, establishing deadlines, networking, and devoting time, effort, and money to your goals.

The Rewards of Making Proactive Steps towards Your Goals

Taking the initiative to achieve your goals has a number of rewards, including:

1. **Enhanced Clarity:** By acting, you'll become more aware of your goals and what has to be done to fulfill them.
2. **Momentum:** Taking action builds momentum, which inspires additional action and advances you closer to your objectives.
3. **Overcoming Difficulties:** You'll face difficulties and setbacks as a result of taking action, which you can use to grow and develop.
4. **Building self-assurance and self-worth:** Taking action increases self-assurance and self-worth, which can help you succeed better in other aspects of your life.
5. **Achieving Results:** In the end, taking action is what helps you to get the results you want.

The Typical Pitfalls of Passivity and Procrastination

Although it's simple to become enthused about our aspirations and make goals, putting them into action is quite another. Typical pitfalls of passivity and procrastination include:

1. **Worry of Failure:** Because they are worried about failing or making mistakes, many people are reluctant to act.
2. **Lack of Clarity:** It's easy to feel overwhelmed and unclear about what to do next without a defined roadmap or action plan.
3. **Perfectionism:** Because they want things to be perfect before they begin, some people become trapped in the planning stage and never take action.

4. **Temptations:** Countless temptations and diversionary activities, such as social media, Netflix, and menial work, might prevent us from acting.
5. **Lack of Accountability:** It's easy to let ourselves off the hook and put off completing a task in the absence of a support network or accountability partner.

❧

Defining Your Desires and Set Precise Goals

You must be aware of what you actually want before you can take steps to make your desires a reality. Many people struggle to define their desires precisely while having a general concept of what they want. It's critical to precisely define your goals and aspirations since doing so will help you stay motivated, focused, and on track. In this section, we'll discuss how to develop SMART goals, how to connect your aspirations with your beliefs and purpose, and the importance of clarity and precision in goal-setting.

The Role of Clarity and Specificity in Goal-Setting

Lack of clarity and specificity in goals is one of the main causes of people's failure to fulfill their desires. You need to be clear and specific about what you want; having a general idea is not enough. Making an action plan and moving toward your goals is easier the more clarity and precision you have.

You can maintain your motivation and focus by being clear and specific. You're more likely to stay motivated and focused on the actions you need to take to reach your goals when you have a clear idea of what you want. Your chances of success increase with the clarity of your goals.

How to Make Your Desires Complement Your Values and Purpose

Complementing your desires with your values and purpose is a crucial part of establishing your desires and setting clear goals. Your wants are built on your values and purpose, so complementing them can help you set goals that are both meaningful and fulfilling.

Asking yourself what matters most to you will help you complement your desires with your beliefs and purpose. What are your guiding principles, and how do they align with your goals? What is your life's mission, and how may your desires aid in achieving it?

Creating SMART Goals: Specific, Measurable, Attainable, Relevant, Time-bound

A potent strategy for transforming your aspirations into attainable targets is to set SMART goals. Specific, Measurable, Attainable, Relevant, and Time-bound is the acronym for SMART. Setting clear, attainable, and inspiring objectives requires each of these components.

Specific

> *"Goals should be specific and unambiguous, with no opportunity for doubt or misunderstanding. Making an action plan and taking steps to achieve your goals are easier the more specific they are."*

Measurable

"*Goals should be measurable so that you can monitor your development and gauge your progress. Measurable goals give you a sense of accomplishment as you reach milestones and keep you motivated and focused.*"

Achievable

"*Achievable goals are ones that are both difficult and practical. You won't be inspired to strive toward your goals if they are too easy, and you'll lose motivation if they are too difficult.*"

Relevant

"*Your objectives should be relevant to your desires, your values, and your life's purpose. You'll find it difficult to remain motivated and focused if your goals don't reflect the things that are most important to you.*"

Time-bound

"*Your goals should include a deadline or time range so that you feel accountable and under pressure to complete them. Setting time-bound goals enables you to organize your efforts and make sure that you are moving closer to your objectives.*"

Getting Past Challenges and Reluctance to Take Action

Even when your goals and ambitions are well-defined, it can be difficult to take the necessary steps to make them a reality. It might be challenging to advance when there are challenges and resistance present. In this section, we'll look at some typical roadblocks to action and how to get beyond them, including recognizing the fear of failure and success, seeing limiting beliefs and self-talk, growing resilience, and developing a growth mindset.

Taking steps to realize your goals can be hampered significantly by fear. The fear of failure and the fear of success are two frequently encountered phobias. Failure anxiety may be crippling, making you mistrust your skills and unable to take chances. On the other side, the fear of success can also be a hindrance since it makes you anxious about the potential changes that can result from attaining your goals.

To overcome the fear of failure and success, it's important to understand the underlying reasons behind these fears. For example, fear of failure may be rooted in perfectionism or past experiences of criticism or rejection. Fear of success may be rooted in self-doubt or a fear of the unknown.

Negative self-talk and limiting ideas might also prevent you from acting on your aspirations. Being motivated and maintaining focus can be challenging when one holds onto these self-defeating beliefs and thoughts.

Start by recognizing your limiting thoughts and self-talk in order to overcome them. When you consider taking action to fulfill your desires, pay attention to the thoughts and beliefs that come into your head. Are they adverse or favorable? Are they constructive or destructive? Once you've found them, put them to the test by calling into doubt their veracity and then swap them out for uplifting and powerful ideas.

You can overcome obstacles and resistance to action by cultivating resilience and a growth mindset. A growth mindset is a conviction that your skills and abilities can be improved with effort and commitment. It's the conviction that obstacles might present chances for development and education. The ability to overcome obstacles and setbacks and to persevere in the face of adversity is resilience.

Focus on the act of moving toward your goals rather than the result in order to foster a growth mindset and resilience. Accept obstacles and failures as chances for development and learning. Celebrate your accomplishments and learn to be kind to yourself. Be in the company of uplifting and motivating people who can hold you accountable and provide encouragement.

Taking Regular and Coordinated Action

The next phase in manifesting your wants is to take regular and coordinated action. This is done after you have defined your desires, established clear goals, and conquered any hurdles or reluctance to action. We'll discuss the significance of making a daily or weekly action plan, taking tiny, consistent steps toward your goals, and making sure that your actions are in line with your aims and values in this part.

Taking tiny, regular movements in the direction of your objectives is one of the most crucial things you can do to actualize your wishes. This is so because sustained action generates momentum and increases self-assurance. Your ambitions will seem less overwhelming if you divide them up into smaller, more doable activities.

You're also more likely to stay motivated and avoid burnout when you make tiny, regular progress toward your goals. This is because you're concentrating on one step at a time rather than trying to tackle everything at once.

Making a daily or weekly action plan will help you make sure you're moving toward your goals consistently. This plan should outline precise actions or tasks that you can carry out every day or every week to get closer to your goal.

Prioritize the tasks that are most crucial and will have the biggest impact while establishing your action plan. By doing so, you'll be able to maintain your attention on what really counts rather than getting sucked into less significant chores.

Making ensuring that your activities are in line with your aims and values is another crucial component of taking consistent and coordinated action toward your goals. This entails acting in accordance with your true desires rather than what you feel you should do or what other people might demand of you.

It's helpful to think about what matters most to you and what you actually want to accomplish in order to make sure that your actions are in line with your intentions and values. This may entail giving up ideas or actions that are no longer helpful to you and acquiring new routines or ways of thinking that are more in line with your goals.

You're more likely to feel a feeling of purpose and fulfilment and less likely to experience burnout or irritation when your activities are in line with your aims and values. Because you'll understand why you're acting the way you are, you'll also be more inspired to pursue your goals.

Staying Accountable and Motivated

It's crucial to take consistent, aligned action as well as to continue to be accountable and motivated throughout the process if you want to manifest your desires. This entails setting up support networks, monitoring your development, and developing self-control and internal motivation. We'll discuss the advantages of accountability and support networks, how to monitor and assess your progress, and how to develop self-control and intrinsic drive in this section.

When pursuing your goals, having accountability and support networks in place can be quite helpful. Having an accountability partner or joining a group of people with similar interests who can offer support and encouragement are two examples of how to do this.

You're more likely to stay motivated and on track to achieve your goals when you have accountability and support mechanisms in place. This occurs as a result of your sense of belonging and connection, as well as your awareness of the support you get from others.

Additionally, accountability and support structures can aid in your continued attention and discipline because they increase your propensity to follow through on commitments.

Monitoring and evaluating your progress is another crucial component of remaining responsible and motivated. This entails tracking your progress toward your objectives on a regular basis and making necessary adjustments.

It can be beneficial to divide your goals into more manageable, measurable milestones so that you can monitor and evaluate your progress. This will make it simpler for you to reflect on your progress and recognize your accomplishments along the road.

It's crucial to keep tabs on your development in a manner that suits you. This can entail use a monitoring app, a spreadsheet, or a planner. Whatever approach you decide on, make sure it's something you'll actually utilize and that fits your unique needs and goals.

Finally, developing self-control and internal motivation is another aspect of being responsible and motivated. The ability to follow through on commitments and take action even when you don't feel like it is a necessary component of self-discipline. On the other side, intrinsic motivation involves experiencing joy and fulfilment while pursuing your objectives.

Establishing routines that help you achieve your goals and creating boundaries that are clear are essential steps in developing self-discipline. This may entail creating guidelines for how you spend your time or assigning particular duties to certain times of the day.

Focusing on the pleasure and fulfillment that come from pursuing your goals rather than merely the outcome will help you develop intrinsic motivation. Finding ways to make the process more fun or concentrating on the beneficial effects that your activities are having on both your life and the lives of those around you will help you achieve this.

Honoring Your Successes and Improving From Your Mistakes

When working towards manifesting your desires, it's important to not only stay accountable and motivated but also honor your success and improve from your mistakes along the way. In this section, we'll explore the power of gratitude and positive feedback loops, how to learn from setbacks and failures, and the importance of self-reflection and continuous improvement.

Honoring your success is a crucial part of maintaining motivation and moving on with your goals. By taking the time to recognize and appreciate your accomplishments, you're establishing a constructive feedback loop that can assist you in gaining momentum and maintaining motivation.

A potent strategy for creating constructive feedback loops is gratitude. By thanking others for your successes, you cultivate a positive outlook that can enable you to find the silver lining in any circumstance. Even in the face of obstacles and losses, maintaining a positive outlook helps keep you inspired and committed to your objectives.

How to Learn from Setbacks and Failures

Failure and setbacks are inevitable on the path to realizing your goals. It's crucial to resist letting them discourage you or sap your willpower, though. Instead, see mistakes and setbacks as chances to improve.

Take a step back and analyze what went wrong to learn from setbacks and mistakes. You could accomplish this by asking yourself, "What could I have done differently?" What did this experience teach me? How can I use this information in the future?

Reframing setbacks and mistakes as learning opportunities rather than failures is also crucial. When things don't go according to plan, this can help you maintain your motivation and focus on your goals.

In addition to celebrating your successes and learning from your mistakes, continuous improvement and self-reflection are also involved. This entails pausing to consider how close you are to achieving your objectives and making necessary corrections.

Asking oneself questions like Am I on track toward my goals? can be a part of self-reflection. What do I need to work on the most? What has this process taught me about who I am and what I want?

Continuous improvement refers to little, gradual improvements that help you move closer to your objectives. This can entail experimenting with different approaches, looking for more assistance or resources, or making adjustments to your regular routine.

₰

The Effects of Taking Initiatives on Your Well-Being and Self-Esteem

You're not just working toward your objectives when you take proactive measures to manifest your wishes; you're also boosting your sense of purpose, self-worth, and confidence. You can improve your general well-being by taking charge of your life and making an effort to achieve your goals. By doing this, you're strengthening a sense of agency and control.

By acting, you can also acquire crucial experience and abilities that can help you become more self-assured and confident. As you move closer to your objectives, you'll start to think more highly of yourself and believe that you are capable of doing even more.

The Consequences of Your Deeds for People and the World

However, the effects of taking action extend well beyond simply you. Your actions may affect individuals close to you as well as the entire planet.

When you take the initiative to achieve your goals, you motivate others to follow your example. You're empowering them to take charge of their own destiny by demonstrating to them that it's possible to make significant changes in their life.

Additionally, the steps you take to realize your goals may have a good influence on the rest of the world. Your actions can significantly impact the lives of others, whether it's by starting a company that creates jobs and boosts the economy or by donating your time and money to a cause you care about.

I want to leave you with some final words of inspiration to act and realize your aspirations. Keep in mind that achieving your goals requires effort and won't always be simple. Along the path, there will be obstacles and difficulties, but these are all chances for improvement and education.

You can design the life you truly want by clearly defining your desires, setting specific goals, overcoming obstacles and resistance to action, acting consistently and in line with your goals, staying accountable and motivated, celebrating your successes and learning from your failures, and understanding how your actions affect both you and the rest of the world.

Take action now and start the process. Start where you are, with what you have, and move forward with your goals instead of waiting for the ideal time or opportunity. You may design a life that is truly gratifying and meaningful if you are dedicated, persistent, and ready to act.

Chapter Summary

- To become a reality, dreams, and ambitions need to be actively pursued. Dreams are just wish if nothing is done with them.
- There are several advantages to taking the initiative to reach your goals, including improved clarity and momentum, conquering challenges, developing self-assurance and self-worth, and getting results.
- Typical problems like perfectionism, lack of clarity, distractions, and lack of accountability can keep us from moving forward with our goals. In order to realize our goals, it is essential to recognize and remove these obstacles.
- Overcoming challenges can be aided by developing resilience and a growth attitude. Focusing on achieving goals, accepting setbacks as opportunities for growth, celebrating successes, being kind to oneself, and surrounding oneself with encouraging people are all ways to nurture these traits.
- Take constant, synchronized action toward your goals, be responsible and driven, and you will attract what you want. Create a daily or weekly action plan and break down your goals into smaller, more doable activities. Make sure your behavior reflects your ideals and aspirations.
- A powerful tactic for transforming aspirations into realizable targets is setting SMART goals. To provide clarity, motivation, and responsibility, goals should be Specific, Measurable, Achievable, Relevant, and Time-Bound.

XI

Feel Your Way to Success

In this chapter, we will examine the role that emotions play in helping us accomplish our goals, as well as how they affect our decisions and the Law of Attraction.

A complex interaction of physiological reactions, mental operations, and subjective experiences makes up emotions. They are frequently referred to as "felt sense," which results from either internal or external stimuli. When something good happens, such as when we accomplish a goal or get a compliment, we may feel happy. Similarly, we also feel sad and anxious if someone criticizes or talks ill about us.

Emotions have a significant impact on our thoughts, actions, and results. Positive emotions like happiness, love, and gratitude increase our propensity to think positively and act positively, which produces favorable results. For instance, we are more inclined to act and persevere in the face of challenges if we feel optimistic and assured about our capacity to accomplish a goal. Thus, our chances of success rise as a result.

On the flip side, when we feel negative emotions like fear, rage, or despair, we are more prone to act and think negatively, which ultimately results in undesirable results. For instance, if we are fearful and unsure about our abilities to complete a task, we can put it off or give up too soon, which lowers our odds of success.

The Relationship Between Emotions and the Law of Attraction

Emotions play a crucial role in the Law of Attraction because they provide the fuel needed to power our manifestation attempts. Positive emotions put us in a high-vibrational condition that encourages good things to happen in our life. Conversely, we are in a low-vibration state when we are experiencing unpleasant emotions, which repel positive experiences and invite bad ones.

Several essential ideas form the foundation of the Law of Attraction. The fundamental tenet is that everything in the cosmos is formed of energy, including our thoughts and emotions, and that everything in the universe is made of vibrating energy. The second tenet is that, whether consciously or unconsciously, we draw into our lives whatever we focus on. The third tenet is that we attract events and experiences into our lives as a direct result of the vibrational energy that our thoughts and emotions produce.

The Law of Attraction states that we can achieve our goals by concentrating our thoughts and feelings more on what we want than on what we don't want. This is predicated on the idea that the universe reacts to the energy that we create and that if we emit positive energy, we will attract positive events and opportunities into our lives.

Aligning our emotions with our intended outcomes is crucial if we want to materialize our desires through the Law of Attraction. This entails nurturing positive emotions that are consistent with our objectives, like joy, appreciation, and enthusiasm, and letting go of unhelpful emotions, like fear, doubt, and concern.

The Science of Emotions

Our ideas, behaviors, and interpersonal connections are all significantly influenced by our emotions, which are a fundamental element of the human experience. A combination of physiological reactions, mental processes, and subjective experiences make up the complex, diverse phenomenon of emotions. This section will examine the science of emotions, including their biology, their function in motivation, decision-making, and learning, as well as the effects of both happy and negative emotions on human success and well-being.

Knowing the Biological Basis of Emotions

The brain, the body, and the environment interact intricately to produce emotions. External stimuli, such as a dangerous circumstance or a joyful experience, frequently cause emotions to arise. Our brains activate a sophisticated network of neural circuits that coordinate a variety of physiological and cognitive responses when we experience emotions.

The limbic system, which comprises organs like the amygdala, hippocampus, and hypothalamus, is at the corner of the brain's emotional processing system. These systems are in charge of handling emotional data and producing emotional reactions. For instance, the hippocampus is involved in the processing of memory and emotion, whereas the amygdala is involved in the processing of fear and other unpleasant emotions.

Emotions entail the activation of several neurochemicals, including dopamine, serotonin, and oxytocin, in addition to the limbic system. These substances are essential for controlling motivation, emotion, and social behavior.

Emotion's Role in Motivation, Decision-Making, and Learning

Motivation, decision-making, and learning are all significantly influenced by emotions. Our behavior is frequently driven by emotions, which have an impact on our decisions and deeds. For instance, the fear of failing can spur us to work harder and take more chances, and the emotion of love and connection can spur us to forge closer bonds with others.

Decision-making is greatly influenced by emotions as well. Emotions give us important information about our surroundings and assist us in assessing the possible effects of various decisions. When making decisions, emotions assist us in weighing the advantages and disadvantages of several options and direct us toward the decision that is most in line with our objectives and core beliefs.

Finally, emotions are crucial for memory and learning. Emotions can aid in the successful encoding and recall of information, and emotional events are frequently more memorable than neutral ones. Students, for instance, are more likely to remember facts that they find intriguing or applicable to their daily life.

The Effects of Good and Bad Emotions on Our Success and Well-Being

Emotions have a significant effect on our success and general well-being. Joy, love, and gratitude are examples of positive emotions that have been connected to a variety of advantages, such as improved physical health, increased resilience, and higher levels of happiness and life satisfaction. Additionally, positive emotions can improve decision-making, problem-solving, and creativity.

On the other hand, unpleasant emotions like fear, rage, and despair can harm our success and well-being. Negative emotions are linked to a rise in stress, anxiety, and depression, as well as a decline in social interaction and cognitive function. Negative feelings can sometimes result in inappropriate behavior, such as anger and avoidance.

Your Emotional Energy

Emotions are a powerful form of energy that can have a major impact on our vibrational energy. We vibrate at a high frequency when we are experiencing strong emotions like joy, love, or gratitude, which attracts other forms of energy. On the other side, negative emotions like fear, hatred, or despair cause us to vibrate at a low frequency, which can encourage more of the same in our life.

Aligning our emotions with our ambitions is crucial if we want to achieve our goals. This implies that we should concentrate on experiencing the feelings we would have if we had already attained our goal outcome. For instance, if we want to manifest a new job, we can concentrate on experiencing the joy, appreciation, and excitement that come with having the position already.

Even when we are not actively experiencing any unpleasant emotions or limiting beliefs, it can be challenging to align our emotions with our aspirations. However, by using strategies like gratitude, visualization, and positive affirmations, we can progressively reorient our emotional energy and position ourselves to achieve our goals.

Identifying Your Desired Emotional State

There is no denying the link between emotions and objectives. Our thoughts, acts, and, ultimately, our results are all influenced by our emotions. Therefore, when defining goals and working toward manifestation, it is essential to determine our intended emotional state. In this section, we'll examine the relationship between emotions and objectives and talk about how to manage our emotions so that they don't get in the way of manifestation.

Setting goals requires taking into account both the desired outcome and the emotional state we wish to experience as a result of that achievement. Consider the emotional state we aspire to acquire through financial achievement, for instance, if our goal is to make more money. This may entail sensations of safety, liberation, and wealth.

Our goals for our lives can become more significant and gratifying if we can pinpoint the emotional state we want to be in. This emotional state can also serve as a guide for choosing our actions and moving toward our objectives.

We might start by thinking back on our current feelings and noting any patterns or themes that emerge in order to clarify our intended emotional state. After that, we might think about the emotional state we want to accomplish through our goals and imagine what that might be like.

To clarify and reinforce our intended emotional state, it can also be beneficial to apply strategies like visualization and positive affirmations. For instance, to change our emotional state in the direction of our desired result, we may repeat affirmations like "I am worthy of abundance and success" or "I am surrounded by love and positivity."

Methods for Controlling and Shifting Your Emotions

Controlling and shifting our emotions can be a difficult but worthwhile skill. We may cultivate a more pleasant and content emotional state, which can help us draw more gratifying events and opportunities into our life. This is done by learning to recognize and control our emotions.

Meditation is one method for controlling and changing our emotions. We may increase our emotional awareness and learn to better control our emotions by keeping our focus on the here and now and monitoring our thoughts and feelings without passing judgement.

Another method for controlling and shifting our emotions is Cognitive Behavioral Therapy (CBT). The goal of CBT is to uncover negative thought patterns, challenge them, and then replace them with more powerful and positive ones.

Last but not least, engaging in good emotion-promoting activities like spending time in nature, expressing one's creativity, or cultivating appreciation might be beneficial.

Cultivating Positive Emotions

A positive attitude is essential to the manifestation process. Positive emotions cause us to attract more possibilities and positive experiences into our lives. In order to achieve our goals, it is essential to nurture and sustain a happy emotional state.

Numerous advantages for manifestation come from positive emotions. First of all, they assist in raising our vibration and drawing more fortunate events and chances into our lives. Second, they boost our general sense of happiness and well-being, which can help us stay motivated and goal-focused. Finally, experiencing good feelings encourages us to adopt a more upbeat and confident perspective, which can be helpful in overcoming challenges and realizing our objectives.

There are several methods we might employ to elicit pleasant emotions like thanksgiving, joy, and love. Practicing thankfulness is one of the best methods for developing pleasant feelings. By concentrating on our blessings, we can divert our attention from unfavourable feelings and ideas and develop a more upbeat and hopeful outlook.

Participating in things that make us happy and fulfilled is another method for developing positive emotions. This could involve engaging in interests, spending time with friends and family, or performing deeds of kindness and service to others.

Finally, developing love and compassion for both ourselves and others can also be a powerful approach to producing happy feelings. Self-love and self-compassion exercises can help us develop a more upbeat and empowering perspective, which can be helpful in attaining our objectives.

Ways of Maintaining a Positive Emotional State Despite Setbacks and Challenges

It can be difficult to keep an optimistic outlook on life, especially when we encounter obstacles and disappointments along the way to our objectives. Even in the face of difficulty, there are methods we may employ to keep a happy emotional state.

One strategy is to concentrate on the lessons and development possibilities that result from difficulties and failures. We may maintain a more upbeat and empowering mindset by shifting our perspective and emphasizing the positive aspects of trying circumstances.

Participating in activities that encourage relaxation and stress alleviation, such as mindfulness exercises, yoga, or meditation, is another strategy. These activities can support a more positive emotional state by lowering stress and anxiety.

Finally, asking for aid from friends, family members, or a therapist or coach might be beneficial. We can learn fresh perspectives and insights as well as innovative techniques for sustaining a pleasant emotional state despite obstacles and challenges by talking through our struggles and feelings with others.

ॐ

Dumping Negative Emotions

Our manifestation process can be significantly impacted by negative emotions. There is a saying, "You reap what you sow." When you feel sad all the time, do not expect results that will make you feel happy. You cannot expect apples when you plant potatoes. When we feel unfavorable emotions like fear, wrath, or doubt, we draw more unfavorable possibilities and events into our lives. Negative emotions cause us to generate a lower frequency of energy, which draws more unfavorable opportunities and events into our lives. In addition to making it difficult for us to stay motivated and focused on our objectives, negative emotions can also prevent us from achieving our goals. It is crucial to understand how to dump unpleasant emotions and go over limiting ideas and emotional barriers.

Methods of Dumping Negative Emotions

We can utilize a variety of methods to dump unfavorable feelings, including fear, rage, and doubt. Acknowledging and accepting your unpleasant feelings is one of the best ways to let them go. When we recognize and accept our negative emotions, we may start to let them go and refocus on more uplifting feelings.

Exercise or movement is another method for letting go of unfavorable emotions. Exercise and movement can aid in the body's release of tension and unfavorable feelings, fostering a more positive emotional state.

Negative emotions can also be effectively released through mindfulness and meditation techniques. We can start to let go of negative emotions and develop a more upbeat and tranquil mentality by keeping our attention on the here and now and monitoring our thoughts and feelings without passing judgment.

Ways of Overcoming Limiting Beliefs and Emotional Blocks

Our ability to realize our goals might also be hampered by limiting beliefs and emotional blocks. We all have limiting beliefs, which are ideas we have about the world or ourselves that limit our potential and keep us from attaining our objectives. Negative emotions that are strongly embedded in our subconscious minds are known as emotional blocks, and they can stop us from achieving our goals.

We must first recognize our limiting ideas and emotional barriers before we can get past them. Identifying negative thought and behavior patterns and reflecting on our feelings will help us achieve this.

We may start to confront and redefine our limiting ideas and emotional barriers after we have identified them. We can accomplish this by challenging the veracity of our beliefs and reinterpreting them in a way that is powerful and constructive. For instance, if we think we can't accomplish our goals, we might challenge this notion by seeking evidence to the contrary and rephrasing it as a more optimistic notion, like "I can accomplish my goals if I work hard and stay focused."

Finally, by developing a more optimistic and empowering perspective, we can get over limiting beliefs and emotional barriers. This can be achieved by concentrating on encouraging thoughts, expressing thanks, and partaking in self-love- and self-care-promoting activities.

Chapter Summary

- Our thoughts, acts, and outcomes can all be affected by emotions, which are a strong force in our life.
- According to the Law of Attraction, in order for our desires to manifest successfully, we must bring our emotions into harmony with our goals.
- Emotional alignment and manifestation depend on knowing what emotional state we want to be in and taking action to foster positive emotions while letting go of negative ones.
- The emotional manifestation process requires both taking inspired action and having faith in the process.
- Daily rituals like appreciation, visualization, self-care, and surrounding ourselves with inspiring people are necessary to stay in alignment with our aspirations and sustain a healthy emotional state.
- Limiting beliefs and emotional blocks can hinder our ability to achieve our goals. We need to identify and challenge negative thoughts and beliefs and cultivate a positive perspective to overcome these obstacles.

XII

Release and Receive

Many of us have probably heard or read about this manifestation technique—the "letting go"—somewhere. However, many individuals are perplexed because they believe that letting go entails giving up on one's goals and aspirations. *How, therefore, are we to let go of what we so desperately want? This is absolutely not possible.* At first, it may not be easy to understand the concept at first, but if you want to actualize your goals, you must comprehend this idea.

"Letting go does not really means letting go of your desire to travel to a specific place, the desire to marry that specific person, etc. Instead, it is letting go of and letting go of your attachment to things that are preventing you from attaining your goals, such as limiting beliefs, unfavorable emotions, and outdated

behavioral habits."

Why is letting go so important to achieving your goals? Considering that when you cling to these constricting ideas and emotions, you build energetic barriers that prohibit the universe from sending you what you genuinely want. By removing these obstacles, you make room for fresh, uplifting energy to enter your life.

We'll delve deeper into the idea of letting go in this chapter and explain why it's crucial for attracting your desires. We'll also go through a number of methods you can employ to let go of constricting thoughts, feelings, and actions, and we'll look at examples of people who have used these methods to materialize their dreams in real life.

This chapter will provide you with the tools you need to let go of what's restricting you and make room for the abundance you want, regardless of how experienced you are with the concept of letting go. So, let's explore the power of releasing and receiving now!

Understanding Letting Go

It's critical to investigate what letting go implies and how it functions in order to appreciate its power properly. In essence, letting go is relinquishing control over how something will turn out and allowing it to develop naturally. Many individuals may find this challenging since we frequently feel the need to exert control over every element of our lives in order to make sure that things go our way. This demand for control, though, might sometimes get in the way of our achieving our goals. We could cling to unfavorable thoughts or feelings that are obstructing the flow of positive energy, or we might be emotionally invested in a particular result that keeps us from being flexible.

Attachments of all kinds, such as emotional attachments, attachments to the past, attachments to a particular result, etc., can prevent manifestation. We cannot acquire what we actually want because of the energetic blocks that these attachments produce.

Attachments to particular feelings, such as dread, doubt, or concern, can keep you from feeling upbeat and confident about the conclusion you want. People frequently hold on to outdated notions based on their past experiences. Holding on to outdated ideas, memories, or connections that stop you from progressing can be one way this manifests. You can lock yourself up to other options and hinder your ability to manifest what is actually in your best interest if you become overly obsessed with a particular outcome at times. For instance, if you are too emotionally invested in the concept of a particular job or promotion, you may unintentionally obstruct other options that would be a better fit for you. You can be hindering yourself from discovering true love and connection if you are attached to a particular outcome in a relationship.

Holding onto unfavorable thoughts and feelings might also prevent your desires from materializing. These are ideas that you have about yourself or the outside world that prevent you from living up to your potential or achieving your goals. For instance, if you continue to believe that you are unworthy of success or love, you will continue to draw circumstances that support that idea. You will draw more situations that make you feel angry or resentful if you harbour anger or resentment toward someone.

It's critical to recognize and bring to the surface these attachments and beliefs in order to release them. Only after that can you start to let them go and make room for good energy to enter your life. We'll look at several methods for letting go and releasing these energetic obstacles in the section that follows.

&

Paybacks of Letting Go

Although letting go can be difficult, the benefits are immeasurable. You make room for positive energy to enter your life when you let go of your attachment to negative thoughts and feelings. Just a few advantages of letting go include the following:

Eliminating resistance: Losing attachment to a certain result can help you feel less resistant to it in the future. Letting go can make you more receptive to receiving what you want because resistance can keep you from getting it.

Lowering anxiety and stress: You can lessen stress and anxiety associated to attaining your goal when you let go of the need to control the outcome. Your wellbeing as a whole will increase, and you'll feel happier as a result.

Letting the universe do its thing: By letting go, you give the universe the freedom to fulfil your desires. This indicates that you are open to getting your goal in ways you may not have anticipated and that you are not restricting the methods in which it can come to you.

Living in the moment: When you let go, you concentrate on the here and now and what you can do right away to make your situation better. This can assist you in acting on your goal without becoming overly dependent on the result.

Believing in the process: Letting go might make it easier for you to have faith in the law of attraction and trust that what you want is coming to you. This can assist you in maintaining a happy attitude and high vibration, both of which are necessary for drawing in the things you want.

When it comes to the power of letting go, these advantages are merely the tip of the iceberg. We'll discuss several methods for letting go that you may use right away to start reaping these advantages in the following section.

Methods of letting go

You can utilize a variety of methods to let go of unfavorable thoughts and feelings and make room for positive energy to enter your life. Some of the best methods for letting go are discussed below:

Meditation and mindfulness practices can help you increase your awareness of your thoughts and feelings and teach you how to observe them objectively. This can assist you in recognizing and letting go of unhelpful thought and emotion patterns. You might realize, for instance, that you frequently reflect on your errors from the past or worry unnecessarily about the future. You can start to develop a more balanced and present-focused viewpoint and start to let go of unhelpful negative thoughts and emotions by being aware of these tendencies.

Journaling is a powerful tool for self-reflection that can assist you in identifying unfavorable feelings and ideas that are restricting your progress. It can be easier to let go of a situation if you can put your ideas and feelings into writing. Writing can also help you gain perspective and clarity on a problem. Journaling can also assist you in gaining perspective and understanding of a circumstance. Writing about your experiences gives you the opportunity to take a step back and look at the situation from a fresh perspective. You may be able to see things more clearly as a result, which may make it simpler for you to let go of your bad feelings and go on.

Forgiveness is an effective technique for getting rid of unfavorable feelings and ideas. Forgiving individuals who have wronged you or yourself may be included in this. You can make room for self-love, self-acceptance, and self-improvement by forgiving yourself in order to let go of self-talk, self-doubt, and self-blame. Keeping resentments and grudges towards other people might make you feel emotionally and psychologically exhausted. You are not endorsing the behavior of those who have injured you when you forgive them; rather, you are freeing yourself from the unfavorable feelings and ideas connected to that hurt. You can let go of unpleasant feelings and make room for uplifting energy to enter your life by practicing forgiveness.

Affirmations and visualization can assist you in programming empowering thoughts and feelings into your subconscious mind. While visualization is forming an internal picture of what you want to materialize, affirmations are encouraging remarks that you repeat to yourself. These methods can assist you in letting go of unfavorable thoughts and feelings so that you can make room for positive energy to enter your life. Affirmations and imagery work well together as potent tool for personal development and change. They can assist you in reimagining your world as one that is positive, prosperous, and joyful. You may break free from negative thought patterns and design a life that is genuinely gratifying and rewarding by reprogramming your subconscious mind with positive thoughts and feelings.

These are just a few of the numerous methods you can employ to let go of unfavorable thoughts and feelings and make room for the inflow of positive energy. Regular application of these strategies can help you develop a more optimistic outlook and draw in the abundance you actually seek.

Law of Attraction and letting go

Like attracts like, according to the powerful principle known as the Law of Attraction. This means that comparable situations and individuals will come into your life as a result of the thoughts and beliefs you hold in your mind. The Law of Attraction is based on the idea that we are all energy beings and that the vibrational frequency of our thoughts and emotions attracts events and circumstances that are in tune with that frequency.

Letting go enables you to let go of negative thoughts and emotions that may be preventing positive energy from entering your life, which is a critical step in the manifestation process. Holding onto unfavorable thoughts and feelings raises your vibratory frequency, which draws more unfavorable things into your life. You can develop a more positive vibratory frequency that draws positive experiences and people into your life by letting go of negative thoughts and emotions.

People who have let go of their attachment to particular results and let the universe work its magic are real-life examples of people who have effectively attracted their desires by letting go. Some of them include:

J.K. Rowling

When she began writing the first Harry Potter book, J.K. Rowling was a struggling single mother. She had no idea if it would be a success, but she was fiercely committed to the narrative she had developed. She put aside her uncertainties and worries and carried on with the book. The Harry Potter series is currently among the best-selling in history.

Michael Phelps

One of the most successful Olympic athletes of all time is Michael Phelps. He succeeded by putting his fear of failing aside and concentrating on his objectives. He let go of any negative ideas or doubts that might have been holding him back as he saw himself winning races.

Steve Jobs

Steve Jobs lost his job at Apple, the business he built, but he didn't let it stop him. After letting go of his resentment and aggravation, Steve used the experience to found a new business called NeXT, which eventually brought him back to Apple and allowed him to design some of the most well-known products in history.

Jim Carrey

Prior to becoming a well-known actor, Jim Carrey wrote himself a check for $10 million that was payable in five years. He carried the check and imagined himself as an accomplished actor. Later, he put the check out of his mind and concentrated on his acting profession. He obtained a gig that paid him exactly $10 million five years later.

Overcoming the Resistance to Let Go

Letting go is a crucial aspect of life that many people find difficult. The process of letting go of something that was once an important aspect of our life can be challenging, whether it's a relationship, a career, a belief system, or even a tangible asset. Here are some typical reasons why people find it difficult to let go, techniques for doing so and enjoying the letting go process, as well as the significance of patience and self-compassion in this process.

Reasons for resistance to letting go include:

Fear of the unknown: Because they are afraid of the unknown, many people find it challenging to take the initial step toward letting go. Even though their current circumstance is not ideal, they may be content with it because at least they know what to expect. Giving up a familiar object can feel like leaping into the unknown without knowing where you'll land. Future uncertainty can be a potent force that prevents people from moving forward. They can ponder whether they are making the proper choice or whether they will come to regret it. Another frequent justification for resistance is fear of failure. A common concern is that if someone let go of something, they won't be able to bear the consequences or find something better to replace it.

Attachment: When we talk about attachment, we are referring to the bond or connection we have with something or someone. This link can be established by positive memories, experiences, and connections with others. Attachments to objects, people, places, and even ideologies are common in human beings. An item we are attached to can be difficult to let go of, especially if it has been a part of our lives for a long time. It's possible that psychological, material, or emotional elements contributed to this problem.

Comfort zone: People who feel confident in their current situation could find it challenging to let go. They may not want to take risks or leave their comfort zone. But even though letting go can be terrifying, it can also be liberating and lead to new opportunities for achievement. We give ourselves a chance to discover new interests, make new connections, and embark on new adventures by taking a chance and stepping out of our comfort zone.

Identity: Because they identify with what they are holding on to, people may find it difficult to let go. Identity is a complicated and diverse idea that includes many facets of a person's life, such as their views, values, experiences, and interpersonal relationships. Numerous elements, such as our upbringing, culture, socialization, and personal experiences, influence how we feel about ourselves. As a result, our identity is a dynamic, ongoing process rather than a fixed entity. People frequently believe that letting go of something would alter who they are and their identity.

Guilt: An emotional roadblock that frequently stands in the way of people letting go of someone or something in their lives is guilt. This guilt may result from a number of factors, such as a sense of obligation or accountability, a concern about disappointing others, or a conviction that letting go is a sign of frailty or failure. For instance, if a relationship involves family, close friends, or romantic partners, people could feel bad about ending it. Because they think it speaks ill of their character or that they have failed in some manner, they feel bad about leaving a relationship.

Techniques for overcoming resistance and embracing the letting-go process:

Recognizing this resistance's presence is the first step in conquering it. It's critical to acknowledge the feelings and ideas that surface when you consider letting go of something. This may involve a sense of attachment to the familiar or feelings of anxiety or uncertainty about what the future may hold. It's crucial to look more deeply at the feelings and thoughts that are causing your resistance once you've identified them. Asking yourself: What am I terrified about in particular? What am I holding onto in the circumstance I'm resisting? Are my apprehensions or attachments supported by facts or conjecture?

Consider the advantages of letting go. Think about the advantages of letting go of what you are holding on to. It may result in improvements to your mental clarity, emotional well-being, productivity, relationships, level of self-awareness, personal development, physical health, and other beneficial traits.

The process of letting go of something or someone can be challenging and emotionally taxing. A wide range of emotions, such as grief, rage, and perplexity, are common. It is crucial that you surround yourself with people who can assist you throughout this time. Finding emotional support from friends and family who have your best interests in mind can be really helpful. They can offer you a shoulder to weep on and a listening ear, which can help you process your feelings.

We can be setting ourselves up for failure when we try to let go of something all at once. The size of the change we're trying to accomplish can make us feel overburdened, nervous, and agitated. Instead, it is preferable to start modest and increase gradually. As we advance, this strategy can increase our confidence and make us feel more in charge. For instance, if we wish to end a relationship, we might begin by confining our contact with that person to a certain period of time or location. We might also start looking into new pursuits or interests unrelated to our romantic connection.

Additionally, remember to be kind to yourself as you let go. It's common to experience emotions and have a hard time letting go of something that once had a lot of meaning for you. Letting go is not always easy and can take some time. It's important to be fair to yourself and allow yourself the time and space needed to finish the process. Self-compassion is also crucial in this process. Don't berate yourself for experiencing particular sentiments; instead, be gentle to yourself. Don't rush it; remember that letting go takes time.

Chapter Summary

- It's essential to let go of attachments to constricting thoughts, unfavorable feelings, and outmoded behaviors in order to manifest your goals and allow uplifting energy to flow into your life.
- Eliminating resistance, reducing worry, allowing the universe to work, being present, and believing in the process are some advantages of letting.
- You can utilize methods like forgiveness, affirmations, and visualization to let go of negative thoughts and emotions and make room for positive energy.
- Negative thoughts attract more negativity into your life by raising your vibrational frequency.
- Due to attachment, comfort zone, identity, guilt, and the fear of the unknown, letting go can be challenging. But it can also result in fresh chances for development and success.
- Recognize resistance, accept your emotions, think about the benefits of letting go, get emotional support, start small, and be nice to yourself.

Conclusion

Now that you've reached the last section of "The Science of Achieving Your Desires," I want to take a moment to reflect on the journey we've taken together. We've discussed using your mind's power to realize your potential and fulfill your deepest desires.

We've spoken about setting objectives and breaking them down into manageable steps throughout this book. We've talked about the value of self-awareness and how to develop a positive outlook in order to get past setbacks. In addition to discussing the many manifestation strategies, we've also underlined the importance of action in reaching your goals and how to create positive habits that will keep you inspired and on track.

But let's be honest - The path to fulfilling your goals is not always straightforward. You'll experience disappointments, difficulties, and times when you doubt yourself. It's critical to keep in mind that these challenges are a necessary component of the process and that they sometimes present chances for development and education.

In actuality, your tenacity and persistence will determine your success in the end. Whatever happens, you must never lose sight of your objectives or your commitment to moving forward with them.

But here's the thing - Getting what you want takes time and effort. It's a continuous process that calls for ongoing self-evaluation, adaptation, and development. It involves making fresh resolutions and fervently and purposefully pursuing them.

The Science of Achieving Your Desires includes developing an interior sense of contentment and purpose in addition to obtaining exterior accomplishment. Living a life that is in line with your beliefs, interests, and purpose is important.

As you finish reading this book, I hope that you feel motivated and inspired to take steps to achieve all of your desires. It's important to keep in mind that the journey will be worthwhile even if it's not always simple. Continue to make progress, maintain your goals in mind, and have confidence in your abilities.

I thank you from the core of my heart for sharing this journey with me. As you pursue your deepest desires, may you keep developing and prospering.